Nordic Film Classics

METTE HJORT AND PETER SCHEPELERN, *Series Editors*

NORDIC FILM CLASSICS

The Nordic Film Classics series offers in-depth studies of key films by Danish, Finnish, Icelandic, Norwegian, and Swedish directors. Written by emerging as well as established film scholars, and where possible in conversation with relevant film practitioners, these books help to shed light on the ways in which the Nordic nations and region have contributed to the art of film.

Ingmar Bergman's The Silence: *Pictures in the Typewriter, Writings on the Screen*, by Maaret Koskinen

Dagur Kári's Nói the Albino, by Björn Norðfjörð

Lone Scherfig's Italian for Beginners, by Mette Hjort

Lukas Moodysson's Show Me Love, by Anna Westerståhl Stenport

Thomas Vinterberg's Festen *(The Celebration)*, by C. Claire Thomson

Roy Andersson's Songs from the Second Floor: *Contemplating the Art of Existence*, by Ursula Lindqvist

Roy Andersson's
Songs from the Second Floor
CONTEMPLATING THE ART OF EXISTENCE

Ursula Lindqvist

UNIVERSITY OF WASHINGTON PRESS
Seattle and London

the modern language initiative

THIS BOOK IS MADE POSSIBLE BY A COLLABORATIVE GRANT FROM
THE ANDREW W. MELLON FOUNDATION

Publication of this book also was made possible in part by grants from the
Barbro Osher Pro Suecia Foundation and Gustavus Adolphus College

© 2016 by the University of Washington Press

20 19 18 17 16   5 4 3 2 1

All rights reserved. No part of this publication may be reproduced or transmitted in any
form or by any means, electronic or mechanical, including photocopy, recording, or any
information storage or retrieval system, without permission in writing from the publisher.

UNIVERSITY OF WASHINGTON PRESS
www.washington.edu/uwpress

LIBRARY OF CONGRESS CATALOGING-IN-PUBLICATION DATA
Names: Lindqvist, Ursula.
Title: Roy Andersson's "Songs from the second floor" : contemplating the art of
   existence / Ursula Lindqvist.
Description: Seattle : University of Washington Press, 2016. | Series: Nordic film
   classics | Includes bibliographical references and index.
Identifiers: LCCN 2015047751 | ISBN 9780295998244 (hardcover : alk. paper) |
   ISBN 9780295998251 (pbk. : alk. paper)
Subjects: LCSH: Songs from the second floor (Motion picture) | Andersson, Roy—
   Criticism and interpretation.
Classification: LCC PN1997.S63338 .L55 2016 | DDC 791.43/72—dc23
LC record available at http://lccn.loc.gov/2015047751

The paper used in this publication is acid-free and meets the minimum requirements
of American National Standard for Information Sciences—Permanence of Paper for
Printed Library Materials, ANSI Z39.48–1984.∞

"BELOVED ARE THEY WHO SIT DOWN?!"
Lasse Nordh
1936–2011
In Memoriam

Contents

Acknowledgments	ix
Introduction: A Troublesome Avant-Gardist Stages a Comeback	3
1 Aesthetics: *Film as Art*	19
2 Production: *Film as Industry*	45
3 Intermediality: *Film, Poetry, Painting, Music*	76
4 Humanism: *Film as Philosophy and Social Critique*	119
Epilogue: *Songs Carried On*	150
Appendix: Roy Andersson's Eclectic Oeuvre	155
Notes	163
Bibliography	175
Index	189

Acknowledgments

I first saw *Songs from the Second Floor* in the autumn of 2000 at Slottsbiografen, the old art theater in Uppsala where Ingmar Bergman's grandmother used to take him to matinees. At the time, I was a U.S. Fulbright Fellow at Uppsala University conducting research for my doctoral dissertation in comparative literature, and while I'd taken graduate-level film courses and grown up in the film metropolis of Los Angeles, I had no intention of becoming a film scholar. But Roy Andersson's film exploded my notions of what a film can, or should, be. Its images haunted my thoughts, much as the deceased Sven haunts his friend Kalle in the film, long after I'd returned home and completed my doctoral training as a scholar of poetry and nationalist cultures at the University of Oregon.

In 2004, while a Visiting Lecturer at the University of Illinois at Urbana-Champaign, I was asked to teach a course on Swedish Film, and I put *Songs from the Second Floor* on the syllabus so my students and I could tackle it together. Looking for a way to teach a film with such an unconventional structure, I began by comparing Andersson's remarkable film language to the modernist poetry of César Vallejo, to whom the filmmaker dedicates the film. Professor Rochelle Wright observed my class lecture, was fascinated by how Vallejo's poetry could inform a reading of Andersson's film, and urged me to continue my investigation in the form of an article. Once it appeared in January 2010, I started hearing from colleagues that they'd found it helpful in teaching Andersson's work in their own courses, and I realized that the importance of this filmmaker, and of his enigmatic 'comeback' film, is far greater than the surprisingly little scholarship published on them in English might suggest. This led me to contribute a book on this film to the University of Washington Press' Nordic Film Classics series. I am deeply grateful to series editors Mette Hjort and Peter Schepelern, as well as to Jacqueline Ettinger, former acquisitions editor at the University of Washington Press, and to current editors Larin McLaughlin and Whitney Johnson, for this opportunity.

Most of the research interviews for this book were conducted in Sweden during early summer 2010. At that time, Roy Andersson and his crew at Studio 24 had just begun conducting screen tests for *A Pigeon Sat on a Branch Reflecting on Existence*, which would complete the humanist trilogy that began with *Songs from the Second Floor* and win the Golden Lion at the Venice Film Festival in August 2014. It is impossible to imagine more gracious and generous hosts than Roy Andersson and his team, who made themselves available for interviews; helped me contact amateur actors who had been part of a film made more than ten years earlier; oriented me to how they work at Studio 24; and provided high-definition film stills and invaluable archival materials, from early project descriptions and draft scripts to production details. When I returned home, Roy Andersson's conviction that the trivial and the monumental cohabit everyday life became all too real, as it proved an enormous challenge to complete a thoughtful manuscript while also giving birth to, and raising, a child; coping with loved ones' inevitable aging and illness; designing and teaching six college courses a year; co-editing two critical anthologies; and moving my family from big-city Boston to small-town St. Peter, Minnesota. I thank all whom I interviewed for this book, as well as the University of Washington Press, for their patience. Hopefully, having had more time to reflect on a film that was, after all, twenty years in the making has resulted in a much better book.

Deepest thanks are due to Roy Andersson, István Borbás, Jesper Klevenås, Pernilla Sandström, Jane Ljung, Johan Carlsson, and Peter Cohen at Studio 24; former Studio 24 producer Lisa Alwert; amateur actors Stefan Larsson, Eva Stenfeldt, and Gunnar Ivarsson; and Lars ("Lasse") and Margot Nordh, who hosted me at their summer home in rural Småland so that I could interview Lasse, who played the unforgettable Kalle in the film. Lasse passed away in December 2011, and although he will never read this book, I dedicate it to his memory. Thanks are also due to composer Benny Andersson, filmmaker Ruben Östlund, and Pia Lundberg, head of Swedish Film Institute's International Division, for their invaluable insights. Nearly all interviews for this book were conducted in Swedish, and I have translated them into English in quoting them here.

I have also benefit from the able assistance of archival librarians and research assistants, in particular Ola Törjas at the Swedish Film Institute Library; the staff at the National Library of Sweden's sound and picture archive; Doris Sperber, faculty research assistant in the Department of Germanic Languages and Literatures at Harvard; Sonja Timmerman, head of the Interlibrary Loan division at Gustavus Adolphus College; Administrative Assistant Jenny Tollefson and her student worker bees; and the interlibrary loan staffs at the University of Colorado at Boulder, UCLA, and Harvard's Widener Library. Nearly all archival material referenced in this book is in Swedish, and I have translated it into English in quoting it here.

For invaluable and incisive feedback on the ideas presented in this book, I offer profuse thanks to the anonymous reviewers of this manuscript, as well as Shelley Wright, Ellen Rees, Marilyn Miller, Andrew Nestingen, Arne Lunde, Laura Horak, Kendra Willson, Peter Elmore, Josh Overcast, Tom Dolack, Nandini Dhar, Peter Burgard, John Tucker, Eduardo Ledesma, Rachel Willson-Broyles, Kathy Saranpa, Julianne Yang, and students in my Nordic Cinema courses at Harvard and Gustavus. I am especially grateful to Tim Roberts and Kerrie Maynes of the Modern Language Initiative, who helped prepare the manuscript for publication. For mentorship and support, I thank Elissa Guralnick, Mette Hjort, Reiland Rabaka, Stephen Mitchell, Linnea Wren, Tim Tangherlini, Nandini Dhar, Tracey Sands, Lisa Parkes, Jill Locke, Kjerstin Moody, Glenn Kranking, David Jessup, Marian Frazier, and Yurie Hong. The Kendall Center for Engaged Learning, as well as Paula O'Loughlin, Thomas W. Young, Mark Braun, and Lisa Heldke, helped me secure the critical time, space, and resources needed to complete this book. Thanks also to the Kienholz family, the Träskelins/Wesshagens, and to Caitlin Sandborg for logistical support, and to Gaywyn Moore for friendship, wit and wisdom, and writing tips.

For research and publication funding, I am deeply thankful to the Barbro Osher Pro Suecia Foundation, Gustavus Adolphus College, the Swedish Institute in Stockholm, and Harvard University's Department of Germanic Languages and Literatures.

This book could not have come to fruition without the unflagging support of extended family and friends, for whom I am ever thankful. My deepest and most heartfelt thanks are for my husband and daughter, whose presence in my daily life helped me learn, as I sat and wrote this book, the weight of Vallejo's words, "Beloved is the one who sits down."

January 2015

Roy Andersson's

Songs from the Second Floor

Introduction: A Troublesome Avant-Gardist Stages a Comeback

It is hard to imagine a single film as long anticipated as Roy Andersson's *Songs from the Second Floor* (*Sånger från andra våningen*, 2000). As the *Guardian*'s film critic Jonathan Romney later noted, "The 25 years between his second and third features make Andersson cinema's champion absentee, beating even Terrence Malick and Victor Erice" (2001). Leading up to the Cannes International Film Festival in 2000, with Swedish media abuzz over whether the notoriously meticulous director would finish editing the film in time to enter it in the competition, many film journalists were skeptical that *Songs* could live up to the hype that had been building for decades—partly fueled by the director himself, who, as Swedish critic Mats Weman put it, "had been so busy sitting in sofas on cultural programs and harping on the importance of 'the complex image'" (2000a). In his film reportage leading up to Cannes, Swedish journalist Mattias Göransson recounts an exchange he had with a VIP in the Swedish film industry he simply calls "G":[1]

I asked how he could be so certain that Roy Andersson's film would be "the Swedish film event of the decade."

"Because it will be," he replied.

"But the expectations are so high," I countered. "Even if the film is good, it need not be a masterpiece, and that would be enough for it to be seen as a flop."

"That's just it," G said. "The biggest success or the biggest fiasco—it doesn't matter. The film will be the Swedish film event of the decade no matter what." (2000, 10)

In May 2000, *Songs from the Second Floor* won the Prix du Jury, among the world's top film prizes, at the Cannes Film Festival. In February 2001 it went on to dominate Sweden's "Oscars," the Guldbagge ("Golden Bug") Awards, and the Swedish Film Institute chose it as Sweden's entry into the Oscar competition for Best Foreign Language Film over several strong contenders: the Ingmar Bergman–scripted *Faithless* (*Trolösa*), directed by Liv Ullmann; and Lukas Moodysson's *Together* (*Tillsammans*).[2] Andersson reveled in the vindication. *Songs from the Second Floor* proved the ultimate comeback film for Andersson, who was fifty-seven, and whose debut feature *A Swedish Love Story* (*En kärlekshistoria*, 1970), released when the director was only twenty-six, had won him international acclaim, awards, and meetings with Hollywood producers—only to be followed by three decades on the margins as Sweden's most infamous film pariah.

For the embattled director, the win at Cannes symbolized the film industry elite's embrace not only of his groundbreaking film but also of Andersson's unique vision for film. For Andersson, *Songs* was never intended to be the culmination of anything—and certainly not of his own film career. Rather, *Songs*, released at the dawn of the new millennium, signaled the feature debut of a radically new film language, one so unprecedented and unfamiliar that some questioned whether it could be called a film at all. "Roy Andersson's film is neither a film nor a classic and least of all those two words together," Swedish film critic Håkan Lahger pronounced after the film's premiere (2000, 24). Most critics, however, heralded the film as the pioneering work it was—including the late great American critic Roger Ebert, who later chose the film to be screened at his 2002 Overlooked Film Festival (also known as Ebertfest.). "I love this film because it is completely new, starting from a place no other film has started from, proceeding implacably to demonstrate the logic of its despair, arriving at a place of no hope," Ebert wrote in a review published on his website. "You have never seen a film like this before. You may not enjoy it, but you will not forget it" (2002).

This book, accordingly, situates Andersson as a paradoxical filmmaker. On the one hand, he has unquestionably become a distinctive auteur with a signature filmmaking style. On the other, he has long worked as a troublesome avant-gardist, crafting scathing critiques of both the film industry in which he works and the powers that be in Western society in the twenty-first century—an age marked by global economic recessions, the resurgence of radical nationalism in Europe, and much hand-wringing over the beleaguered Nordic welfare model. In his book *Our Time's Fear of Seriousness* (*Vår tids rädsla för allvar*, 1995), written after *Songs* was conceived but before filming began in 1996, Andersson argues that a new, more deliberate and "serious" kind of filmmaking was needed to articulate critiques of modern society:

> The aesthetics and narration that, almost without exception, characterize today's film and television industry are rarely deliberate and show few signs of clear thinking. This style is above all a film language of makeshift solutions, lack of time, laziness,

incompetence and avarice, and it bears many resemblances with the way our society, indeed the entire world, is being analyzed and governed. (2009, 40)

In contrast to the kind of rushed, ill-considered narratives Andersson critiques in his polemic, *Songs* offers viewers a lethargic, ponderous film, one that not only ruminates visually on the state of mankind but also forces the viewer to choose where to look within each scene. Not only is editing, used in conventional film narratives to ease the viewing experience by directing our gaze, entirely absent within scenes, but Andersson also composes each shot as a "complex image" with no clear-cut focal point (as I discuss in the first chapter). As film historian David Bordwell argues in *Figures Traced in Light: On Cinematic Staging* (2005), even in cinema's earliest days, when longer takes and less editing was the norm, directors would compose their shots to direct the viewer's gaze within the frame. In a 2007 blog post, Bordwell underscores the strangeness of Andersson's dramaturgy: "How can I not like a filmmaker so committed to moving his actors around diagonal spaces, even if the frame is either sparse or uniformly packed, and though he does treat people like sacks of coal? . . . I'm drawn to directors who create a powerful visual and auditory world more or less out of phase with reality as we usually see it (in life and in movies). Andersson is one such director" (Bordwell 2007).

In a global film industry dominated by high-tech experimentation, Andersson has striven to perfect techniques associated with classic silent cinema. The first such technique is trompe l'oeil, or optical illusions, favored by film pioneers such as Georges Méliès but largely made obsolete by recent digital filmmaking technologies such as Computer Generated Images (CGI). Other techniques include sight gags and dramatic irony, most strongly associated with the silent films of Charlie Chaplin and Buster Keaton (as I discuss in chapter

3). Visually speaking, Andersson's sets are inspired by the simplicity and muted hues of Germany's Neue Sachlichkeit, or New Objectivity, a movement in the arts and philosophy that immediately predates the Second World War (as I also discuss in chapter 3). Andersson's appropriation of older art forms places him in step with the European avant-gardists of the early twentieth century, most notably the dadaists, who tended to reach back to "primitive" and "pure" forms of art for inspiration. This same generation of avant-gardists were also almost universally opposed to war and created new forms of art as an outcry against war, dehumanization, and (in the case of the surrealists) automation in modern life, despite the fact that the term "avant-garde" itself is the French word denoting a military's front line, the one that suffers the most casualties but clears the way for the advancing army. (This opposition to war also characterizes Andersson's work, as I discuss in later chapters.) In an artistic context, avant-garde art tends to incite heated debate among artists and cultural authorities at the moment of its debut, but neither the ideas nor the art typically gains a mass following. Rather, avant-garde art tends to inspire a handful of true believers who seek to emulate rather than imitate it—which has also been the case with the film trilogy that *Songs* began.

In his essay "What Is Avant-Garde?" Richard Kostelantz writes that "avant-garde art usually offends people, especially serious artists, before it persuades. More precisely, it offends not in terms of subject *but as art*; most of its audience cannot believe that art is made in this way or are reluctant to accept that perhaps it can be [emphasis added]" (1982, 15). Few have questioned whether *Songs from the Second Floor* is art; in fact, even critics who panned the film extolled its unforgettable images. (One notable exception is the award-winning Swedish filmmaker Lukas Moodysson, who famously said the film "reminds me of my own poetry when I was 17 years old," called it banal and pretentious, and booed and left the gala when it was awarded Sweden's top film prize; Krutmeijer 2014 and Edgar 2001). Indeed, the two most common complaints Andersson has heard about the film are that it is "pretentious," implying that it purports to be something more than it actually is (Oscarsson 2013), and that it isn't a real film, in the sense that it doesn't function the way a conventional film does.[3] In other words, much to Andersson's dismay, those who have criticized *Songs* have attacked its artistic claims and largely been silent on the societal critiques it advances.[4] And while interns have flocked to Andersson's Studio 24 to learn his method, *Songs* has hardly inspired mass experimentation or imitation in the way that, for example, the Dogma 95 movement has done (see Hjort and MacKenzie 2003). Andersson's unique film aesthetics have, however, made an imprint on a new generation of Nordic filmmakers.[5] In an interview following the release of his film *The Bothersome Man* (*Den brysomme mannen*, 2006), Norwegian filmmaker Jens Lien openly acknowledged Andersson's influence (Pham 2007). Similarly, Swedish filmmaker Jens Jonsson's *The King of Ping Pong* (*Ping pong-kingen*, 2008), which won the Jury Prize at the 2008 Sundance Film Festival, draws heavily from Andersson's painterly hues, long shots, and framing of human subjects in social spaces. Swedish filmmakers Henrik Hellström's and Fredrik Wenzel's highly acclaimed film *Burrowing* (*Man Tänker Sitt*, 2009), also bears traces of this aesthetic. But the filmmaker who has acknowledged his debt to Andersson most openly is Ruben Östlund, who grew up in Andersson's own hometown of Gothenburg watching Andersson's famous commercials. Östlund was formally introduced to Andersson's ideas about filmmaking while studying film at the University of Gothenburg's Valand Academy, which awarded Andersson an honorary doctorate in the aftermath of his 2000 Cannes triumph (and where Andersson's longtime colleague, producer Kalle Boman, is on the faculty). Östlund has adopted Andersson's techniques of the fixed camera, long takes, long shots, and trivial moments and dialogue in all of his films: *Guitar Mongoloid* (*Gitarrmongot*, 2004), *The Involuntary* (*De ofrivilliga*, 2008), *Play* (2011), and *Force Majeure* (*Turist*, 2014). But even Östlund says Andersson's stubborn refusal to provide a narrative structure loses some viewers. "If you make a feature film, you have to consider that you're dealing with a *föreställning*—a show," Östlund said in an interview in January 2015. "I don't think that he has been very interested in that. And that's a problem for him, because sometimes there are extraordinary scenes that don't get the right attention."[6] In fact, Andersson pays excruciatingly close attention to the film's superstructure, which he builds through a progressive repetition of images, dialogue, and music rather than through conventional narrative techniques (as I discuss in chapter 3). But the fact that even filmmakers who warmly acknowledge artistic debts to Andersson remain perplexed by his method underscores his perpetual avant-garde status, long after he has reinforced his position as a global auteur.

Indeed, the English-language press materials that *Songs*' Swedish distributor, Triangelfilm of Malmö, prepared for international festivals sheds little light on what to expect from the film. Presumably because the film has no conventional plot to summarize, the introductory description on the first page takes the form of a philosophical, free verse poem instead:

One evening, somewhere in our hemisphere,
a strange series of events take place:
a clerk is made redundant in a degrading manner;
an immigrant is violently attacked in the street;
a magician makes a disastrous mess of his
number. . . . In the midst of this mayhem one

person stands out—it is Karl and his face is covered in ashes. He has just put a match to his furniture store to get the insurance money. No one can get a wink of sleep that night. The following day the signs of pending chaos are starting to be felt as the madness grips a board of directors and the city itself is paralysed by a horrendous traffic jam. While at the beginning of the millennium, everyone is losing it, Karl is gradually becoming conscious of the absurdity of the world and realises just how difficult it is to be human . . . (Triangelfilm 2000)

A more helpful introduction to Andersson's work might be to prepare the viewer as to what to expect from his distinctive filmmaking style and what motivates it, which is exactly what this book is intended to do. Andersson's hallmarks include a fixed camera that does not move within a scene; wide-angled shots that frame human figures in their spaces; long, single takes for each scene; studio sets that use trompe l'oeil to give the perception of spatial depth; minimalist and monochromatic set designs; an ensemble of amateur actors in whiteface; sight gags and dramatic irony; banal and truncated dialogue; a lethargic pace; and a superstructure that edits together a series of thematically related vignettes—cinematic *tableaux vivants*—in place of a single edited narrative. *Songs* consists of forty-six such vignettes—essentially minifilms that sometimes feature characters we've already met and sometimes introduce entirely new ones. Together, Andersson says, all of the characters represent various aspects of the archetypal human being, and the ninety-eight-minute film amounts to a rumination on the state of mankind at the turn of the twenty-first century.

Andersson has continued making films in this vein, releasing a single feature film every seven years. He shrugs off a common complaint that his films are too much alike; as I discuss in chapter 3, repetition is key to his aesthetic and critical strategies. Andersson further insists that his work is no more repetitive than that of other filmmakers and that the distinctiveness of his style makes his repetitions impossible to gloss over or absorb as easily. "I assume that it is much more obvious, with a pronounced style, when you repeat it, and that causes irritation," he said in a television interview with Swedish talk show host Ann-Marie Rauer.[7] *Songs* thus became the first installment in a humanist trilogy of films that Andersson continued in 2007 with *You, the Living* (*Du Levande*) and completed in 2014 with *A Pigeon Sat on a Branch Reflecting on Existence* (*En duva satt på en gren och funderade på tillvaron*). The third film in the series won the Golden Lion at the Venice Film Festival—the first Swedish film ever to do so. "I think that when we look back 50 years from now at these works, we're going to wonder what kind of person this was who had entirely his own film language and made films as no one else did, films that avail themselves of film's potential in an excellent and fastidious way," cultural correspondent Roger Wilson of Swedish Radio said during a September 2014 broadcast from the Venice Film Festival.[8]

In the years since *Songs* appeared, filmmakers the world over—among them British filmmaker Mike Leigh, US filmmakers Lana Wachowski and Darren Aronofsky, and Mexican filmmaker Alejandro González Iñárritu—have credited Andersson with breathing new life into the film medium. As I discuss in the first chapter, Andersson's use of concentrated, long takes with a fixed camera aligns him artistically with a new generation of global filmmakers reviving a "docufictional" style, first made popular in the 1960s, that uses documentary techniques to depict social problems in feature films. *New York Times* film critic Dave Kehr notes that Andersson's embrace of such long takes is shared by international filmmakers associated with the "slow cinema" movement, among them China's Jia Zhang-ke

(*Still Life*, 2006), Argentina's Lisandro Alonso (*Los Muertos*, 2004), and Portugal's Pedro Costa (*Colossal Youth*, 2006).[9] Kehr writes, "It's a method that seems to have arisen as a counterbalance to that hyperkinetic editing that dominates Hollywood, in which a series of short, tight shots is used to focus the audience's attention on plot details (and to provide an ostensibly pleasurable retinal buzz)" (2010). Unlike the average Hollywood film, and contrary to critic Lahger's assertion that "few are going to die of longing to re-watch *Songs from the Second Floor*, tomorrow or in ten years," *Songs* has unquestionably earned a permanent place in Nordic and global film history, not only for the remarkable tale of how it got made in the first place but also for its audacious claim to have revolutionized the art of filmmaking and the language of film. "He is highlighting the triviality of existence in a better way than anyone else," Östlund said in a 2015 interview. "I have so many times in my life thought that, 'This is a Roy Andersson scene that I'm in right now.' And that is the best, how do you say, *betyg* [testament], that he has actually widened the perspective of my life, so suddenly I can really enjoy something that is kind of trivial, or just stupid."[10]

While *Songs* was rankling in Andersson's mind for decades, ultimately it took four years of filming and cost fifty million Swedish crowns—an unprecedented amount for a Swedish film.[11] It was an epic attempt to make good on a claim Andersson had made, without irony, to Swedish media after his celebrated 1970 debut that he would make an even better feature, one that would be "the best film in the world." As journalist Anna Bell Dahlberg wrote, "He said it completely calmly and self-evidently, and hard-core skeptics were at least convinced of one thing: Roy Andersson's belief in his own talent" (Dahlberg 1976, 23). Europa Films, which had signed Andersson to direct *A Swedish Love Story* when he was still in film school, initially signed on to produce the second feature he proposed, titled

Two Brothers and a Sister (*Två bröder och en syster*), then backed out right before filming was to start, saying that Andersson's ambitious plans for a three-hour philosophical film poem shot in Panavision were too costly for the studio. Andersson resigned himself to making a different film, *Giliap* (1975), for the large Swedish production company Sandrew Film & Teater instead; however, he soon became frustrated trying to impose his vision for a new film language in an industry environment that seemed to him rigid, pedantic, and hopelessly conventional. The result was a film that overran both its production schedule and its budget. Critics, bewildered by the film, panned it, and it flopped at the box office. Andersson, who had taken on personal debts to complete the film, filed for bankruptcy.[12] In the years that followed, despite film critics' favorable reevaluation of *Giliap*, Andersson was unable to secure financing from the Swedish Film Institute to make the kind of films he wanted to make. So instead, he turned to making advertising films. By 1981, he had earned enough money to buy a building at Sibyllegatan 24 in downtown Stockholm that had once housed a pawnbroker's shop. He moved himself into one of the building's apartments, rented out the others, and turned the old storefront into an independent film studio, Studio 24. In the years that followed, as his reputation grew and he began winning international awards for his advertising films, Andersson invested heavily in equipping his film studio with everything he needed to make art his own way, without having to follow anyone else's rules. The "second floor" from which his film's "songs" emanate is thus not a constructed space within the film itself but rather Andersson's living and working spaces on the second floor of the Sibyllegatan building. In effect, *Songs from the Second Floor* grew out of Andersson's twenty-year battle for the space and the resources to develop the language of film in a new way. This proved a daunting task in a state-supported domestic film industry that seemed to want only two kinds of filmmakers: those who made films as popular entertainment, and those who made global art films like Ingmar Bergman's (1918–2007).

Andersson is emphatically neither. He remains a paradox in the Nordic film industry, celebrated both for award-winning "anti-advertising" films featuring products from ketchup to insurance and for "high art" feature films that are intensely critical of Western capitalist society. While his critical art features have rendered him a global auteur, it is his droll advertising films featuring everyman characters that are best known to mass audiences in Sweden and Scandinavia (see Brodén 2014). These paradoxes originate in Andersson's childhood in Gothenburg, where he grew up in a working-class family with dreams of becoming an author. His father, a potato salesman, was among the contingent of Swedish soldiers sent to guard the border with Norway during the Second World War. Andersson himself was born in 1943, during the war's later years, and as I discuss in the coming chapters, this historical period has placed a time stamp on his allegedly timeless and universal films. While Andersson today lives and works in Östermalm, a high-end neighborhood of Stockholm right down the street from the National Library of Sweden, he has not attempted to shake off the experience of growing up a member of the urban underclass in Sweden's second-largest city. In interviews, he has often reminisced about the Swedish welfare society of his childhood in Gothenburg, when the municipality treated working-class children like him to trips to the beach and free buns with milk (Oscarsson 2013). Andersson's persistent advocacy, through his writings and his films, for socially committed art that highlights the plight of the powerless and agitates for a more just world has earned him a number of prizes established in honor of working-class Swedish authors.[13] Little wonder, then, that the film he admires most is Vittorio De Sica's *Bicycle Thieves* (*Ladri di biciclette*, 1948), to which he gave homage during his acceptance speech at the Venice Film Festival when he was awarded the Golden Lion for *A Pigeon* in September 2014. *Bicycle Thieves* chronicles how a man's loss of his bicycle—the mode of transportation he needs to work—sends his family into a spiral of poverty and desperation. "I feel sort of like one of them in *Bicycle Thieves*, that is, the proletariat, the underclass," Andersson said in a 2010 interview. "I don't belong to the underclass anymore, but I have strong experiences from it. So I have my sympathies there the whole time."[14]

Andersson's political and class sympathies placed him at odds with Bergman once Andersson began his studies at the Swedish Film Institute's Film School (called simply Filmskolan) in Stockholm in the turbulent 1960s.[15] "In film school, first I filmed only anti-Vietnam demonstrations," Andersson recalled in a 2013 interview. "This resulted in my being summoned by Ingmar Bergman, who was the managing director. Bergman said, 'If you keep this up, I'll see to it that you never get to make a feature film'" (Oscarsson 2013). But Andersson was undeterred; he soon joined a group of leftist filmmakers called Grupp 13—among them Boman and Bo Widerberg—to make the controversial documentary *The White Sport* (*Den vita sporten*, 1968), which chronicled the intense protests surrounding the Davis Cup tennis match between Sweden and the African state of Rhodesia (then an apartheid regime occupying the area that today is Zimbabwe) in Båstad, in southern Sweden. Harry Schein, legendary head of the Swedish Film Institute (SFI) for much of the 1960s and '70s, sought to censor the film, which ultimately premiered to rave reviews and won the Chaplin Prize awarded by SFI's official film magazine. In his 1980 self-titled memoir, Schein names Andersson as the most "aggressive and confused" filmmaker among the Swedish film industry's leftist contingent (Klinthage 1991). Andersson, for his part, recalls Schein as "a poor subservient slave" to the

Swedish cultural establishment, over which Bergman reigned supreme (Oscarsson 2013). One of the other students at the film school while Andersson was there, the award-winning documentary filmmaker Stefan Jarl, who also comes from a working-class background, said later that Andersson stood out in an industry dominated by bourgeois perspectives. "[He] brought something new to that House of Bergman," said Jarl, who was infuriated by Bergman's assertion, in his series *Bergman's Twentieth Century* (*Bergmans 1900-tal*), that Andersson was too focused on perfecting images and not concerned enough with humanity in his films. "It was *people* Roy brought with him!" Jarl said in Göransson's reportage on the making of *Songs*. "It was people, but from another class than Bergman. It was working-class people—but Bergman didn't see them" (Göransson 2000, 80).

Over the years, Andersson has maintained a deeply ambivalent relationship to the Swedish film establishment, where he is admired for his talent but also resented by some for his perceived arrogance (Weman 1998, 20–30). Indeed, even during the decades when he had dropped out of feature filmmaking, Andersson penned opinion pieces sharply criticizing what he considered the moral and artistic vacuity of Swedish cinema. In the Swedish Film Institute's journal, *Chaplin*, and in his own book, *Our Time's Fear of Seriousness*, Andersson condemns the Swedish cultural establishment for failing to challenge young directors to make complex films that challenge the status quo. Instead, he writes, it encourages a market-driven professionalism that reflects the provincial anxieties of a small national cinema in the global marketplace. "Film reform today," Andersson wrote in the 1995 edition of *Our Time's Fear of Seriousness*, "along with significant portions of the Swedish television industry, is responsible for the achievement of letting the Swedish people pay with public money for their own growing stupidity" (Roy Andersson 1995, 80). Andersson is also not afraid to take aim at Swedish cinema's sacred cows: he has famously called Bergman "overrated" and lacking humor, even while he acknowledges that the director put Swedish film on the global map and expresses admiration for three of his films (out of the forty-eight features Bergman made during his lifetime): *The Silence* (*Tystnaden*, 1963), *Winter Light* (*Nattvärdsgästerna*, 1963), and *Persona* (1966).[16] Despite his anti-Bergman protestations, however, one could argue that certain visual traces from Bergman's films can be found in *Songs*; for example, the film's multiple asylum scenes arguably evoke *Persona*, and the parade of flagellants can't help but conjure *The Seventh Seal* (*Den sjunde inseglet*, 1957) for many cinephiles. But the only Swedish film director for whom Andersson expresses unchecked admiration is Bo Widerberg (1930–1997), who also championed working-class themes in films such as *Ådalen 31* (1969) and *Joe Hill* (1971) and published a treatise, *Vision in Swedish Film* (*Visionen i svensk film*) in 1962 that condemned the Swedish film industry for being overly insular and mummified.[17] Like Widerberg, Andersson believes that a great film is inherently political, but not didactic. It is inspired by great humanist thinkers and resonates with viewers irrespective of class or level of education. The images are complex, but the ideas are simple and universal. It is both tragic and comic. And most of all, while a great film meets the highest artistic standards, it is—as the dedication page of *Our Time's Fear of Seriousness* declares—"for everyone."

This book explores the ample paradoxes that infuse *Songs from the Second Floor* and inform its afterlife as a Nordic film classic. It provides behind-the-scenes accounts of the film's earliest conceptions, of the motley crew of mostly young, relatively inexperienced film workers and amateur actors who toiled four long years to bring it to fruition, and of the unconventional methods of a scrappy film studio that has become a mecca of sorts for both burgeoning and established filmmakers. It explores in depth the artistic components that make Andersson's film language so unique. It examines the intermediality that forms the basis of Andersson's distinctive film language, crafting cinema from a blend of poetry, painting, still photography, and music. It investigates the humanist ethos that informs every frame of the film, with inspirations from Peruvian modernist poet César Vallejo (1892–1938) to French antibourgeois writer Louis-Ferdinand Céline (1894–1961) to Austrian-born Israeli Jewish philosopher Martin Buber (1878–1965), as well as the omnipresent specter of the Second World War and its brutal legacies of human greed, genocide, and apathy. And finally, this book situates *Songs from the Second Floor* in its time and place, as an art work intensely critical of both its immediate sociohistorical context—that of the small nation of Sweden—and of the state of humanity as a whole at the dawn of the second millennium.

1
Aesthetics: Film as Art

Residents of Täby, a Stockholm suburb, were bewildered when Roy Andersson's film team took over an old airplane hangar in their town in the summer of 1998 and, slowly but surely, built an entire train station in it—trains, platform, tracks, and all. Then they began hiring extras—more than a hundred of them—outfitted them in nondescript business clothes, and smeared their faces with white makeup. The locals were mystified, but they were happy to join in the production, bring everyone catered lunches, and provide any needed supplies. By the time shooting began, they very much wanted to know what the film was about—and they were astonished by the answer. It was about a man who gets his finger caught in a door.[1]

"I wonder why Roy Andersson built an the entire train station when he could just rent an old station," said one of the extras, face smeared in paint and eating ice cream during a break in filming, in a Swedish television documentary on the making of *Songs from the Second Floor*. "That he builds the entire station for a single shot. Maybe he wants what is real to appear false, and what is false, to appear true. Maybe so!"[2] The extras had many hours to ponder the meaning of it all. Since there are no edits within the scene, everything had to come together perfectly for the entire duration of the shot, which is more than five minutes long and includes a tracking shot—the only scene in the film where the camera moves—toward the end of the scene. It took ample rehearsals and more than a dozen takes to get the scene exactly right. Before the set was built, Andersson had sent members of his team to Prague to survey and photograph the city's central train station, whose features provided a working model for their set design in Täby. The process took two months, which is more than twice the average shooting time typically spent for an entire film in Sweden.[3]

The finished scene, which takes place fifty-one minutes into the film, begins, as real life moments always do, *in medias res*. We hear the echo of commuters' feet approaching on the train platform, punctuated by howls of pain: "Aj aj aj!" The man, presumably a commuter, has slipped and fallen on his way off the train, and his left arm is bent awkwardly behind him, his finger caught in the closed train door. Some commuters gather and speculate about how this could have happened, while others cast mildly curious glances and keep walking. A train conductor kneels next to him and looks up at the window of the closed door, waiting for someone to open it from the inside. The scene, a single take that lasts more than five minutes, is intended to represent the most banal of everyday life moments, and its dramaturgy is intentionally spare and precise, framing the man's misfortune within the social space of the train station. There are no close-ups of the man's facial expression; rather, cinematographer István Borbás places him in the foreground of a long, wide shot that reaches all the way back and up to the arched rear windows of the cavernous station. The man's body is strewn awkwardly across the platform in the lower left corner of the frame, while the other human figures stand around him or walk briskly past to the right, except for the train conductor who kneels stiffly beside him. Most of the commuters, including the man, are dressed in muted gray, black, or gray-blue suits, forming an impression of modern humanity in the mass in its daily commute. The dialogue is sparse and banal, choreographed so that the discussion carries on across the man's sprawled body. As they speak, the commuters address one another, largely ignoring the prone man moaning loudly at their feet:

Commuter 1: [*standing behind the man to the right*] What has happened?
Commuter 2: [*standing in the left foreground*] That's a good question.
Commuter 3: [*standing farther to the right*] He's stuck. He's stuck in the door.
Commuter 1: Well, yes, we can see that, obviously. But how did it happen?
Commuter 2: He slipped, of course.
Commuter 4: [*in the foreground to the right*] Slipped?
Commuter 2: Yeah.
Commuter 4: How clumsy can you be?
Commuter 5: [*an older woman with bright red hair standing next to Commuter 4*] Don't say that. It could happen to the best of us.
Commuter 3: He must have slipped backwards and hit his arm against the door, and it closed on him.
Commuter 1: Yes, but it's clumsy all the same.
Man: Ahhhhhh! (see figure 1.1)

The banal dialogue is inspired by one of Andersson's literary heroes, Irish avant-garde author Samuel Beckett, whose absurdist play *Waiting for Godot* (1949) famously consists entirely of two men doing

1.1 "Caught a Finger." Shot in an old airplane hangar in Täby, a city fifteen kilometers north of Stockholm, in summer 1998. For this single scene, Studio 24 built the entire set to make the hangar look like a train station, including the train, tracks, and platform. Photo courtesy of Studio 24; used with permission.

and saying apparently nothing next to a dead tree on a roadside over the course of two acts. Andersson says that the reason he casts amateur actors is that they can deliver these ludicrously simple lines of dialogue "in an extremely truthful way, so that it sounds so ridiculously trivial coming out of their mouths, and at the same time it becomes very comprehensible, universal" (Andersson and Harringer 2000). The two commuters who seem to empathize with the fallen man—the woman mentioned above, and a portly man in a bright blue suit who helps the man up, hands him his briefcase, and dusts him off—are distinguished visually from the others through color (her bright red hair, his suit in a bolder shade of blue with a bright burgundy tie set against it). Andersson explained the rationale behind his meticulous dramaturgy in a 1998 interview with *Film & TV:* "I want the viewer to come to her own conclusions, I don't want to point them out. I point things out in another way, by working very classically with diagonals, colors, and the film's balance" (Weman 1998, 27). The characters in the scene are archetypes, and the entire scene is an abstraction, a representation of an ordinary moment that could, as the red-haired woman says, happen to anyone. For Andersson, the most significant moments of everyday life are the trivial ones—such as catching one's finger in a door. The red-haired commuter in this scene underscores this by pointing to a scar on her own finger, which she explains got caught in a dresser drawer ten years earlier. Metaphorically speaking, this scene testifies that life's most quotidian moments are the ones that shape and define us as human beings. The fact that Andersson built an entire train station to capture this trivial moment on film testifies to its significance.

Andersson calls his distinctive form of filmmaking "trivialism," a moniker that started as a joke between him and his crew.[4] As they began filming *Songs,* Andersson realized just how apt a term it was, and he took to using it in press interviews, as well as in the director's commentary of the DVD released in the North American market. Trivialism, according to Andersson, is motivated by the belief that the most important social and existential questions of our age come into focus in the most trivial, banal, and even absurd moments of everyday life. He explains:

> One describes the world and our existence in their little trivial elements, and in that way I hope that one also can get to the big, enticing, philosophical questions. But how life is, life is of course trivial, we must button buttons, we must zip up zippers, and we must eat breakfast. It is exceedingly concrete and trivial, the whole of our existence. Even for those who are in positions of

power. I like this very much, emphasizing this triviality, because it pushes people down to earth to that place where one actually belongs. (Andersson 2004)

Andersson's definition of trivialism, then, affirms the fundamental equality of all beings in a world brutally divided into hierarchies. He views this style as a natural successor to the poetic realism of New Wave Czech director Miloš Forman and the neorealism of Polish director Krzysztof Kieślowski (especially *The Decalogue* series, 1989), and he has also expressed admiration for the abstraction in Italian film auteur Federico Fellini's films. Filmmaker Lana Wachowski has furthermore compared Andersson to a figure in the Western literary canon known for his sympathetic depictions of society's "little people":

> I instantly felt an association with [Russian author Anton] Chekov and the way that Chekov understands the more dark, more selfish, narcissistic, destructive nature of humanity and yet he never stops loving humanity. And Roy Andersson has the same compassion, the same ability to dissect us and see us for all of our faults and yet is still able to embrace us and find humor and joy in the human condition. (Weintraub 2012)

In artistic terms, Andersson's embrace of an "ism" to define his style, his polemical writings railing against conventional filmmaking, and his films' rejection of the core conventions of his medium all evoke the avant-garde, which Susan Hayward has defined as film that "seeks to break with tradition and is intentionally politicized in its attempts to do so" (2006, 38). Most would agree that this is an apt description of *Songs from the Second Floor*, which not only presents scathing critiques of Western capitalist society in general and Swedish welfare society in particular, but also abandons the narrative structures that had defined feature filmmaking for more than a century.

In a radical departure from mainstream—or what Andersson likes to call "bourgeois"—cinema, the film refuses to anchor its plot in a major dilemma or conflict that the main protagonist must grapple with to develop as a character. In fact, plot, protagonist, and antagonist are all largely missing from the film. Rather, in each scene, Andersson seeks to capture the essence of some human experience—much as a painting or a lyrical poem does—but with a *moving* image. Collectively, the scenes provide a visual survey of the state of mankind. In an unsuccessful funding application to the Swedish Film Institute in 1994, Andersson described the film's structure thus:

> Narratively speaking, *Songs from the Second Floor* breaks with the conventions that have developed within the Anglo-Saxon film epic with their roots in nineteenth century melodrama. It doesn't have a so-called "straight" story with the development of a conflict, plot twists, and resolution, according to set patterns. In *Songs from the Second Floor*, we meet an existence that can neither be apprehended nor surveyed, teeming with human destinies, some of which we come to learn a little more about, and they become the film's main characters. But we will have the experience, not of following these characters, but rather of bumping into them, losing them from sight for a while, then bumping into them again—and again, and again.[5]

Songs from the Second Floor consists of no fewer than forty-six such images featuring an extensive cast of ordinary characters, most of them caught in painful—often painfully comic—moments. Together, Andersson says, they comprise an archetypal human being who is the film's subject. "All of these people represent something that the human being has," Andersson said in an interview. "Many people are needed in order to show how broad the human spectrum is. It isn't enough with just one person."[6] Just as humanity is a perpetually flawed work in progress, in Andersson's view, so the archetypal human being of his films never overcomes obstacles, achieves wisdom, or comes to a happy ending. As Andersson points out, life inevitably ends in death: "There will be no 'happy end' for any of us."[7]

Andersson's assertion that his films' protagonist is a human archetype is what motivates his use of whiteface, a visual effect intended to equalize all of the characters. However, Swedish film scholar Hynek Pallas, whose 2012 doctoral dissertation *Vithet i svensk spelfilm 1989–2010* (Whiteness in Swedish fiction film, 1989–2010) includes *Songs from the Second Floor* among the films discussed, has argued that whiteness in film is often conflated with a failed masculinity. "The man who experiences a loss of position and sees himself threated by women is a common trend in society," Pallas said in a 2012 interview with *Fria Tidningen* in Stockholm. "This feeling of nostalgia and loss—not least for the utopian Swedish welfare society—is represented in films as well, as in *Darling* [directed by Johan Kling, 2007] and Roy Andersson's films" (Borg 2012). Indeed, Andersson has acknowledged that he has been criticized for the film's relative lack of meaningful female roles.[8] As Swedish critic Kristina Lundblad wrote in a review in *Göteborgs-Posten*:

> The Anderssonian human species is uniquely male. One hundred percent of the scenes are about men, men of different kinds. The women featured are divided into two groups—they are dead or wearing negligé. The former don't say much, and the latter lie in bed and 1) wonder why the man comes home so late; 2) asks why he hasn't called; 3) doesn't want him to leave; or 4) carries

on having sex while the good-guy ex-boyfriend she threw out stands on the street outside. (Lundblad 2000)

Two female characters who don't fit these categories are the gyspy woman in the boardroom and the psychologist, both of whom serve as intermediaries for a higher power. Andersson has countered such criticism by saying that the film targets classes of people who wield social and economic power, and at the turn of the millennium, men still dominated these categories in Sweden and the rest of the world. Sweden is known for its policies promoting gender equality, and the country has consistently ranked very high in the World Economic Forum's Global Gender Gap Index (it was fourth in the world in 2014, the latest year for which rankings were available). Women's access to the labor market, family-friendly policies, and a near-equal ratio of elected female and male leaders in Parliament have largely accounted for the favorable rankings.[9] In addition, in May 2015, Swedish Film Institute CEO Anna Serner announced at the Cannes International Film Festival that SFI's pathbreaking initiatives to achieve gender parity among films receiving SFI funding—which constitute the vast majority of Swedish films—had succeeded in less than three years' time. In 2011, the year Serner took the helm, only 26 percent of all state film funding went to female filmmakers; by 2014, half of all funded films were directed by women, 55 percent were scripted by women, and 65 percent were produced by women (Byrnes 2015). (All three films in Andersson's trilogy fall into the last category as their credited producers, Lisa Alwert and Pernilla Sandström, are women.) Despite the success of such initiatives, however, women are on the whole still paid less than men in Sweden for comparable work, and men continue to dominate business and industry elites (see, for example, Sanandaji 2014). *Songs* is a dystopic film, and Andersson believes that the fact that the sidelined women are not the ones calling the shots, but rather the ones asking questions and expressing bewilderment, casts them as a faint, collective voice of reason and sanity in the world of the film.

Pain, Not Pathos

Counter to Bordwell's and Bergman's readings of his films, Andersson says his aim is never to debase or ridicule the down-and-out characters who populate them. He claims that such critiques are rather indicative of the bourgeois sensibilities that have determined what filmic subjects are acceptable since the birth of the film medium. Andersson's films cast a spotlight on banal, painfully real human moments that those who enjoy certain socioeconomic privileges are often buffered from. "The trivial is embarrassing for the cultural establishment," Andersson said in an interview, noting that most filmmakers and critics tend to come from the middle class and are unaccustomed to confronting these kinds of moments so openly—and particularly not in a feature film. "Trivialism—I love it simply because it irritates the middle class," he said, chuckling.[10] At the same time, Andersson believes that elevating trivial moments to the level of high art not only treats them with the honesty and the respect that they deserve but also advances a powerful social critique. Early in the film, for example, there is a scene (which also begins *in medias res*) in which Lasse, a mid-level clerk who has worked for the same company for thirty years, has just been fired. The scene opens in a long, brightly lit corridor lined with doors, all of them ajar and moving just enough to show that many others are watching the drama in the hallway. In the foreground, Lasse—a scrawny, balding man whom we saw earlier at home shining his shoes in anticipation of his meeting with Pelle Wigert, a high-level executive—is on his knees, desperately clinging to the legs of a large and portly Pelle, who just fired him,

1.2 "A Man Is Fired." Shot at Studio 24. Manager Pelle Wigart (Torbjörn Fallström), caught in an "objective" act of human cruelty, looks directly into the camera, meeting the viewer's gaze, as the rank-and-file employee he just laid off, Lasse (Sten Andersson), clutches his leg and wails, "I've worked here for thirty years!" Frame grab.

and begging, "No, no, no!" Pelle, who in a previous scene had told his boss (who was in a tanning bed preparing for a trip to Barcelona) that he thought it was "a shame" (*tråkigt*) to lay off workers, looks around nervously to see if anyone is watching the spectacle and tells Lasse to pull himself together. As Lasse looks squarely up at Pelle, Pelle's gaze jumps nervously all around the corridor and then stares straight into the camera at the viewer (see figure 1.2).

In that moment, the viewer is activated; no longer merely a spectator, the viewer is now a witness of a working man's pain and his boss's discomfort—just like all the other eyes in the corridor. When

AESTHETICS 29

Lasse refuses to let go of his leg, Pelle turns and pulls away, dragging poor Lasse halfway down the hall before Pelle finally breaks free and strides away quickly. Andersson gives Lasse the last word in this scene; even after Pelle closes the door at the end of the hall, we hear Lasse's voice echoing in the hall: "I've been here for thirty years!" Such an excruciating visual treatment of Lasse's degradation, coupled with Pelle's discomfort and the viewer's activation as witness, all conspire to deny us the convenient avenue of catharsis that conventional melodramas have conditioned us to expect. Instead, Andersson traps us into sensing how useless and cruel it would be to pity this clerk who has lost his job. The film theorist André Bazin, whom Andersson credits with most influencing his filmmaking style, describes a similar dynamic at work in de Sica's *Bicycle Thieves,* the film Andersson most admires: "There is no admixture of pity in it even for the poorest or the most wretched, because pity does violence to the dignity of the man who is its object" (1971, 70). Andersson's intent is that we apprehend fully the nature of Lasse's humiliation: A person has just been told he is no longer needed by a socioeconomic apparatus he has served all of his adult life. In today's economy, the essence of what happens to Lasse in this scene happens to millions; it happens all the time. And in a subsequent scene, when a lost visitor happens upon a photo session of a group of coworkers whose division is closing down, we are made to understand that many who were watching the grotesque spectacle through cracked doors are losing their jobs, as well. By reversing the gaze in this corridor scene, Andersson has made us witnesses to a moral crime of which we all are generally aware—how could we not be, given today's headlines?—but choose not to dwell on in our day-to-day lives. Indeed, most of us assume that we are powerless to do anything about it.

The question is, now that Andersson activates us as witnesses and *forces* us to think about it, how do we respond? Feel guilty, flee the scene, and go home to mope, like Pelle? Close the doors, as Lasse's coworkers do? What other options are there? This image, and its questions, conspire with many similarly discomfiting scenes in the film to linger in our minds, spur our thoughts, and foster a sense of shared responsibility, what Andersson calls "guilt toward existence," which I discuss in chapter 4. The firing scene is arguably one of a sequence of metafilmic moments in the film in which Andersson seeks to illuminate the consequences of being a passive observer—a mere audience, if you will—as opposed to a self-aware viewer with an activated conscience. For example, later in the film, in "The Sacrifice" scene, we watch along with thousands of others as a young girl is pushed off the cliff to her death. Andersson arguably fortifies the viewer's connection with the girl by having her emerge from the front of the frame—where we as viewers (i.e., the "we"-camera) is located—as she is escorted on her death walk to the cliff. Before she appears in the frame, we see a doctor and the psychologist walk backwards into the frame, facing us and leading her. Similarly, the film's final shot (see figure 4.4) concludes with Kalle facing us, his back to the stalkers who advance on both him and us. The implication is that this scene—and indeed, the entire film—is not about Kalle's individual guilt catching up with him but about our existential guilt advancing on us.

Andersson's working-class sympathies are reflected in more subtle ways, as well. Amateur actor Lars Nordh, who played the salesman Kalle in *Songs*, pointed out in a 2010 interview that nearly every scene in the film is populated by nondescript people with no speaking lines working on the margins or in the background of the frame, such as a woman vacuuming near the altar when Kalle walks into a church to share his despair with an unsympathetic clergyman. Nordh also remembered Andersson's incisive attention to trivial production details, which Andersson told him were not only about artistry but also about being true to people's experience. For example, Nordh recalled, there was a light switch plate on the wall of an interior set that didn't look right, so the director had a crew member inch it upward until it reached the perfect height visually. "And I stood there and said, 'Roy, surely a light switch plate can't be all that important.' He said, 'No, let me tell you, if no one sees it, then we've succeeded in that scene. But if there is an electrician with a work injury in the audience, that is the first thing he'll look at, where that plate is, and if it isn't in the right place, then it's a crappy film!'"[11] Lisa Alwert, who was Andersson's chief production assistant as well as his romantic partner during the filming of *Songs*, said in a 2010 interview that the elevation of the trivial was far more than an aesthetic style for the director; it was also a worldview that informed his social interactions.[12] For example, Andersson was aware that Alwert's ex-husband, who was a poet, had died not long before the Studio 24 team was to make a trip to the Gothenburg Film Festival before they were to begin filming *Songs*. Right before they got on the train, Alwert's wisdom tooth began to ache, "and I remember that Roy said, 'Oh no! Now this is happening, too!' and I thought, this man is totally crazy, he is comparing my wisdom tooth to my grief!" Alwert, who left the film industry post-*Songs* to become a crane operator, laughed as she recalled the moment fourteen years later. She also recalled that Roy often would pause in his daily work and ask his crew or the amateur actors seemingly trivial questions that showed concern about the details of their lives. "Even in the midst of his daily discipline," she said, "it's like he *sees* you."[13]

Framing People "In Their Spaces"

It was in the 1950s, when the film medium was a mere half-century old, that the French film journal *Cahiers du cinéma* convinced the world that film not only had become an art form but also had its own distinct language—a language of images that transcended national and linguistic boundaries. Over the next few decades, this premise led to the promotion of an elite class of global directors, or auteurs, who had not only mastered this language but also created their own recognizable visual signatures through the use of cinematic mise-en-scène, or the framing and composition of shots. The auteurs anointed during this period included Jean Renoir, Luis Buñuel, Federico Fellini, Andrei Tarkovsky, Alfred Hitchcock, Ingmar Bergman, and Carl Th. Dreyer, among others. The assumption then, which has largely continued to this day, is that one of the most important elements of the language of film, and one that distinguishes it from related arts, such as theater, is the close-up of the human face—a core element in the visual signatures of Bergman and Dreyer, the classic Nordic auteurs with whose films all subsequent Nordic art films have been compared. Bergman's films, and even more so Dreyer's, are homages to the human face, which they considered essential to film's psychological function. Their compositions were further canonized through foundational film theory taught in film schools and programs; Béla Balázcs, for example, described close-ups as "the contemplation of hidden things" revealed through filmic images in *The Theory of Film* (1948), a text still taught today in many a film course. He writes, "Close-ups are the pictures expressing the poetic sensibility of the director. They show the faces of things and those expressions on them which are significant because they are reflected expressions of our own subconscious feeling" (2009, 274).

Andersson's film language rejects these premises entirely. For Andersson, effective mise-en-scène locates the human being in his or her space. "You feel immediately if it's not his room, if he's there—forced to be there, or if by occasion is there. The room tells us much more than the face," Andersson said during a joint appearance with Ruben Östlund at a retrospective devoted to Andersson's work at the Munich Film Festival in 2011.[14] The closer you get to a person, Andersson believes, the further you get from the truth. "The room tells the truth," he said at the film festival. "The people in the room can lie."[15] This is why Andersson has advocated passionately for what he calls "the complex image," a compositional principle that has become influential enough since the release of *Songs* that a translated excerpt from Andersson's 1995 book *Our Time's Fear of Seriousness* was given the title "The Complex Image" and published in 2010 in an English-language scholarly anthology devoted to Swedish film.[16] Such an image consists of a carefully composed shot with depth of field and no clear focal point, so that—as with a Bruegel painting—the viewer must look for what is important and think about why.[17] This ostensibly more "objective" viewing activates the viewer's intellect and her conscience rather than speaking directly to her emotions (ostensibly the aim with a close-up shot). Such viewing demands far more from the viewer, to be sure, and Andersson believes that's a good thing.

One such example from *Songs* is a scene in the emergency ward, which frames a doctor and a nurse in a sterile, clinical environment. The open door behind them, through which a rolling hospital bed in the hall is visible, gives the image visual depth. The middle-aged doctor sits slumped on a chair to the left, reading something and eating a sandwich, ignoring the middle-aged nurse, who stands stiffly in the right of the frame facing the doctor, leaning against the examination table. There is a tray on the table behind the doctor with two cups of coffee and an untouched sandwich—presumably the nurse's. She ignores the food and stares intently at the doctor, her arms crossed. Neither character shows any clear facial expression, but their bodily postures, their positioning in the room, and the untouched food together communicate that the nurse is deeply upset with the doctor, and that the doctor is indifferent toward her. When the nurse finally blurts out, "When are you going to get a divorce?" and the doctor looks up at her impassively, we learn the banal nature of their conflict, one trivialized even further by the appearance, in the doorway, of a patient with a bleeding head wound. This scene exemplifies how Andersson uses framing and composition to create his unique tragicomedy, one Christopher Mildren has described thus: "The complex images in *Sånger från andra våningen* juxtapose elements so that . . . they generate meaning by their satirical contrast" (2013, 149). Humor is thus a vital component of Andersson's "serious" filmmaking, which the director has described as "taking things seriously, doing things properly, getting to the bottom of things, drawing conclusions, making things clear—something that in no way needs to involve a surly expression or the absence of jokes" (Roy Andersson 2009, 23). The absurd contrast of the bleeding patient's acute physical wound and the nurse's banal, emotional wound generates the comedy, while the doctor's indifference to both of them reveals the tragedy. "When two images are allowed to meet," Andersson asserts, "a superstructure is created which adds artistic value as well as information and insights" (Roy Andersson 2010, 274). In this scene, the doctor's nonresponse not only equalizes all forms of human suffering, it also elevates it to the domain of existential pain by showing the harm that human apathy can cause.

Andersson's embrace of "the complex image" defies a cinematic principle popularized first by Soviet filmmaker Sergei Eisenstein and later by classical Hollywood cinema: the notion that montage, or the juxtaposition of images that together create meaning, is best constructed by editing together different shots, often from varying distances, angles, and perspectives. Instead, Andersson embraces an understanding of montage advanced by Bazin, who believed that montage could be accomplished effectively within a single, wide, deep-focus shot through the juxtaposition or overlaying of images within the frame. "Well used, shooting in depth is not just a more economical, a simpler, and at the same time a more subtle way of getting the most out of a scene," Bazin argues in a classic 1967 essay "The Evolution of the Language of Cinema." He continues, "In addition to affecting the structure of film language, it also affects the relationships of the minds of the spectators to the image, and in consequence it influences the interpretation of the spectacle" (1967a, 35). For Andersson, what first exemplified for him the powerful potential of this compositional principle was an etching by the French artist Jacques Callot (1592–1635) titled *The Hanging* (*La Pendaison*, 1633), which he declared in *Our Time's Fear of Seriousness* "has haunted me throughout my life" (Roy Andersson 2010, 274). Callot's image is composed from a distance, so that the viewer can apprehend not only the multitude of limp human forms hanging from ropes in a large tree but also the dozens of live people who are going about their business elsewhere in the frame, ignoring the atrocity above their heads (see figure 1.3). Andersson recounts,

> I was shocked when I saw it for the first time because of its extreme severity and objectivity. It took a long time before I understood what kind of mechanisms made this image in particular awaken the imagination much more powerfully than a close-up. I started to fantasize about the bourgeoisie who stood to the right, the wives there. What are they thinking about? What do they talk about while the execution is going on? It

1.3   Jacques Callot (France, 1592–1635), *The Hanging* (La Pendaison, 1633). Plate 11 in *The Miseries and Misfortunes of War* [*Les misères et les mal-hevrs de la guerre*] series. Etching, 8.1 cm x 18.6 cm. In his book *Vår tids rädsla för allvar* [Our Time's Fear of Seriousness], which features this image on the cover, Andersson calls it "the image that has scared me the most in my life." Etching held at the Art Gallery of New South Wales, which provided the photograph; used with permission.

looked like it was difficult for the condemned people to get up the ladders. Do they climb up themselves or are they carried up? Or are they persuaded by the priest who says 'It is just as well you help out here so that it's over quickly'? It is one of the images that has shaken me because of its distance, its objectivity, its unsentimentality. (Roy Andersson 2009, 29)

Andersson began to find more and more examples of such complex images in paintings, and as I discuss in chapter 3, this is the main reason he finds far more inspiration in art history than in the work of other filmmakers.

Andersson executes such images on film by stationing the camera at the perfect angle, using a 16-millimeter, wide-angle lens with great depth of field, then painstakingly composing a moving image within its frame. Each and every set is built to project an archetypal human environment, and all of the choreography that takes place during the shot's duration is meticulously mapped out, timed, and rehearsed. These complex images necessarily require long takes so that the viewer has time to apprehend them, appreciate their satire, and, ideally, consider their import. The shortest shot in the film—the thirty-ninth, in which a centenarian general alone in the dark in an eldercare home rattles the bars of his iron crib and pleads, "Help!"— lasts for twenty-five seconds, long enough for viewers to squirm in horror at the undignified way this man, whatever crimes he may have committed in his life, must conclude his one-hundredth birthday. This scene does indeed contain visual irony; we learned in a previous scene that this esteemed general and millionaire was an associate of Hermann Wilhelm Goering, Hitler's most senior officer, and while the centurion has never been convicted of any war crimes, he still finishes out his life behind bars. But there is also a certain correspondence to European art films by, for example, Michelangelo Antonioni and Andrei Tarkovsky, for whom "the long take . . . allows scope for a roaming glance and a heightening process of attention over the duration of the shot, usually over limited action and emphasizing *les temps morts*," as Mildren puts it (2013, 148). Andersson's films are always under two hours in length, but these long, slowly developing shots that challenge conventional modes of viewing make them seem much longer. *Songs'* longest shot, the film's concluding scene and among its most complex, is more than six minutes long.[18] In the entire film, there is only one scene in which the camera moves: a tracking shot that concludes the train station scene, the motivations for which I discuss in chapter 4. Such methods run entirely counter to the modes of viewing ingrained by Hollywood, where, as Bordwell writes in *Figures Traced in Light*, "what has gone almost completely unexplored is the unbudging long take." In fact, Bordwell asserts, "Today perhaps the most radical thing you can do in Hollywood is put your camera on a tripod, set it a fair distance from the action, and let the whole scene play out" (2005, 29).

Another crucial component of Andersson's complex images that he borrows from Bazin is his use of spatial depth and layering—or "staging in depth"—within the long takes to create what Julian Hanich has called "hidden dimensions" (Hanich 2014, 37–50). Andersson creates such dimensions, Hanich argues, by placing human figures in nondescript positions within the shot to be discovered gradually, hiding them behind other elements and revealing them strategically, or insinuating the presence of something outside the frame. Such staging is facilitated by the deep-focus cinematography used by Andersson's longtime collaborator, István Borbás, who never has to refocus between various elements in the shot as they emerge to command the viewer's attention. Andersson has consistently espoused Bazin's argument that such complex images activate the viewer not least because they require the viewer to "exercise at least a minimum of personal choice. It is from his attention and his will that the meaning of the image in part derives" (Bazin 1967a, 36). As Mildren puts it, "In such static shots one has to peer intently to divine the meaning of the image, the gaze largely unguided by the auteur, except insofar as a range of visual elements are all offered up for the viewer's discretionary interest" (Mildren 2013, 151). In Andersson's (and Bazin's) view, forcing the viewer to make a choice activates her social conscience in a way that viewing directed by editing does not. But Andersson's tragicomic satire works only if viewers get the joke. Timing is key; Andersson carefully stages his shots to achieve comical juxtapositions that appear to emerge spontaneously.

As Mildren concludes, "In the long takes of *Sånger från andra våningen*, Andersson introduces comic gag points, and consequently the viewer's gaze is in fact quite directed" (149). An excellent example of this occurs in "The Fire Site" scene in which two insurance inspectors question Kalle, the sooty furniture store owner, about a fire that he claims has burned up not only some very expensive inventory but also the records that could prove the inventory had existed. Kalle sits in the foreground on the remaining half of a burned sofa with a single wooden broom resting against it—a comic element, given that it would take far more than a broom to clean the burned-out store—and the insurance inspectors stand to the left, slightly behind him and turned toward him. In the background of the shot, through the store's broken display windows, we can see cars stuck in a traffic jam on the street outside, inching forward jerkily and honking faintly, their sounds and movements echoing Kalle's whining that "everything happens to me" in the foreground. As in many shots in the film, in a method that evokes the work of Danish painter Vilhelm Hammershøi (1869–1916), Andersson uses door and window frames to create frames within frames, or what Bordwell has called "aperture framing" in a cinematic context, to create a layered shot (2005, 106–61). This technique has also been attributed to Dreyer, whose visual correspondences with Hammershøi were the subject of a 2007 exhibition, *Hammershøi i Dreyer*, at the Centre de Cultura Contemporània in Barcelona, Spain (Fonsmark, Palà, and Torres 2007). Andersson often uses such layering to construct his satirical juxtapositions, as this scene exemplifies.

As Kalle moans "Everything has to happen to me, one catastrophe after the other" and proceeds with an account of all of his troubles to the unsympathetic inspectors (who clearly would prefer an account of the inventory), we hear a bizarre chorus of cries approaching from off screen and human figures in the deep background looking at something down the street, off screen to the left. One of those figures turns out to be Stefan, Kalle's son, who steps into the furniture store through the broken window. Kalle tells his son, "These men are from the insurance company—that's what they say, anyway. We'll just have to believe them"—a jab at the inspectors' request for documentation, which Kalle claims is unreasonable. Then all four men turn to behold the stockbrokers on the street who are crying out and flagellating themselves as they walk, which Andersson has said was inspired by a news report about South Koreans who rushed out onto the street and flagellated themselves in response to the Asian stock market crash of the 1990s.[19] "They are fighting for better times," Kalle says to the inspectors, outraged, "and here you stand and quibble over a sofa and a few armchairs!" Here Kalle juxtaposes the monumental and the trivial, but the visual absurdity of the penitent stockbrokers—who seem to believe that flogging themselves in procession will cause stock prices magically to rise—do little to bolster Kalle's already thin claims. Mildren writes that "this reversion to superstition and mass despair is part of a certain medievalism that runs throughout the film, a plague remedy incongruous in the context of the modern European business environment" (2013, 151). But the absurdity of Andersson's image defies its apparent anachronousness, implying that society's leaders today indeed put far too much trust in the mysterious workings of the market, a secular god who has usurped our religious ones. This street demonstration, which also runs through the background of the film's taxi scene (as I discuss in the next chapter), contains a veiled critique of society's leftist activists from the 1960s generation to which Andersson himself belongs. Back in the 1960s, street protests were clearly their domain; in Andersson's turn-of-the-millennium film, superstitious, self-flagellating capitalist cogs have replaced them. To apprehend the satire fully, the viewer is forced to attend to this moving image's multiple visual and aural planes, then to ponder their ironic juxtapositions.

Finally, another distinctive technique Andersson uses to stage in depth is trompe l'oeil (French for "deceive the eye"), a method made famous by French filmmaker Georges Méliès, who generated the metaphor of filmmaker as magician. The magician role is one that Bergman also embraced in his filmmaking, with thematic references to magicians and mirrors used to deceive the eye or create layering effects.[20] Andersson's use of trompe l'oeil, however, is governed not only by the director's desire to stage in depth but also by the practical limitations involved in building original sets for each scene, as I discuss in the next chapter. The scene "Misgivings II, the Departure Hall," for example, features a wide, long shot of a seemingly endless line of people, extending from Pelle and Robert in the foreground to tiny figures in the deep background, struggling to move their overloaded baggage carts forward to the check-in counter. The round ceiling lamps positioned at set distances overhead, reflected against the shining floor, construct the familiar aesthetic of a large, open airport space with long distances to walk with heavy baggage. But the rear of the image is not a physical space at all but a painting. Studio 24's crew painted a wall in such a way that it appears to be an extension of the departure hall, and because the camera stays perfectly still while the characters move, this illusion is fully maintained. The airport scene was staged and shot in the same studio space as the furniture store scene, with the former seeming as cavernous as the latter seems claustrophobic (see figure 1.4). In *Songs*, Andersson even used trompe l'oeil in the final scene, an expansive outdoor shot on the island of Öland, where his crew built a fake road that appears to extend all the way to the horizon within the camera's frame, while in reality the road was only a few hundred feet long (see figure 4.4). They also built a model of a large city on the horizon, under which Kalle has to drive to enter the dump site.

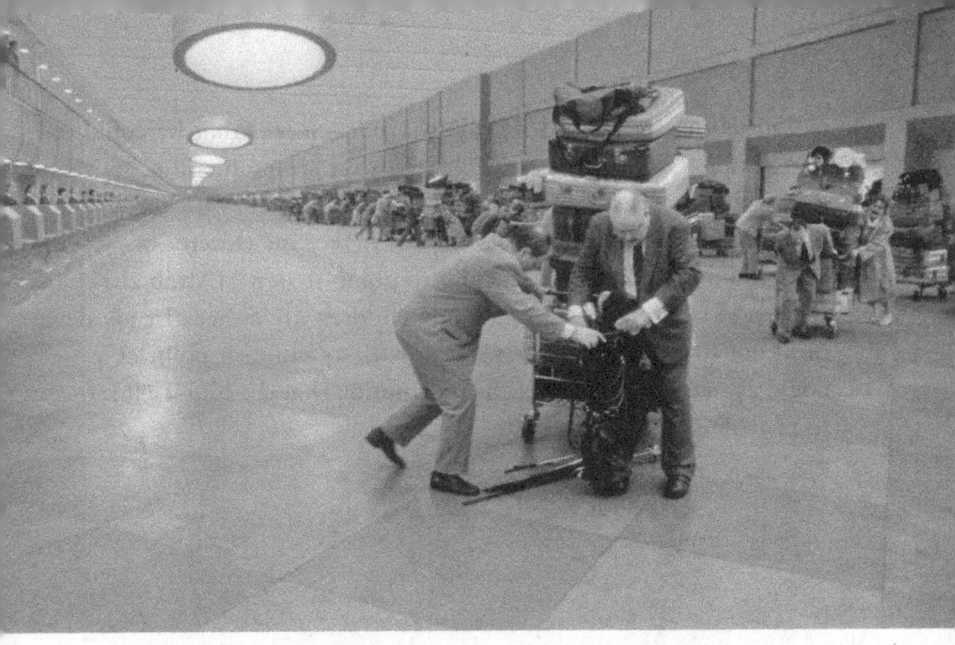

1.4 "Misgivings II—The Departure Hall." Shot in October 1999 at Storängsbotten Studio. This scene is inspired by historical news photos from the Khmer Rouge's takeover of Phnom Penh in Cambodia in 1975, when hordes of people sought in vain to join the American embassy's evacuation in advance of the oncoming army. Andersson uses trompe-l'oeil here to greatly extend the image's depth of field. Photo courtesy of Studio 24; used with permission.

Yet while Andersson has established himself as a master illusionist in the film world, his central aim evokes a modernist credo: to create art that reveals important truths about human existence.[21] Such truth can be reached, Andersson has concluded, only through abstraction; for him, startling, absurd, and carefully crafted abstract images have a greater potential to awaken viewers' intellect and make them ponder life's important questions. By the time Andersson had completed the third film in the trilogy, *A Pigeon*, he'd sharpened his claim, telling the United Kingdom's *Independent* that he could tell that people "are a little more clever" after seeing his film. "It's the same with [Beckett's] *Waiting for Godot*," he said. "It's three hours of banal quarrel and discussion, yet it makes me cleverer because at the end I reach some kind of childish point of view" (Aftab 2015). In the world of *Songs,* where the only children are either already dead or about to be sacrificed, emerging with a "childish point of view" could arguably bring about the redemption that the film itself refuses to provide.

2

Production: Film as Industry

In one of several mental asylum scenes in *Songs from the Second Floor*, Kalle the salesman tells his mute son, Tomas, a patient who had "written poetry until he went nuts," that Kalle had convinced the insurance company to pay up. "You have to be able to speak for yourself—word things in a way that gets results," he tells Tomas.[1] There is ample irony in the scene itself: Tomas, a poet, does not write to "get results" but rather to create art, and in the materialist dystopia of *Songs*, people like Kalle neither value nor comprehend this, which has caused Tomas's psychosis. But this moment also illuminates a paradox about art's economic dimension: art as industry. High-quality art that endures beyond its moment does not usually pay for itself; public and private investment is needed. This is particularly the case in small cinema markets, which can never generate the domestic box office revenues that larger markets can (Hjort and Lindqvist 2016). Sweden's film reform, implemented in 1963, made it possible for production companies to seek public subsidies for thoughtful films that were deemed to have social and artistic value, so as to perpetuate "quality" fare in a media environment transformed by the advent of new entertainment forms such as television

(Timm 2003). Such public investment is meant to ensure the production of high-quality films not only for domestic consumption but also for the international festival circuit, where they compete for awards, facilitate their distribution in foreign markets, and raise the global profile of Swedish cinema. But Sweden's funding mechanisms historically have assumed that filmmakers employ conventional filmmaking methods—starting with the script, then casting actors, and then moving on to production logistics. Swedish filmmakers must, then, learn how to "word things in a way that gets results" to get the funding they need to make their films. Filmmakers who want to try something radically different must convince the funders that their methods will result in high-quality cinema. Anyone familiar with Andersson's twenty-five-year crusade to make films his own way can clearly see that he sides with the poet in *Songs*. But Andersson, unlike the poet, has refused to be silenced. While Andersson's highly unconventional filmmaking methods remain without parallel in the industry, his humanist trilogy that began with *Songs* testifies that it is possible—and even desirable—to make feature films his way. As Swedish film critic Mats Weman wrote in a review in *Nöjesguiden*, "This is a film with such an independent and personal film language that one is prepared to believe that the guy locked himself away from the outside world for the last 25 years. So as not to be influenced" (2000b).

As a young man, Andersson did try to play by the industry's rules when he made *Giliap* (1975), the follow-up to his world-renowned debut film *A Swedish Love Story* (1970). But his artistic ambitions for the film far exceeded the resources and timeline afforded him. For example, the production studio did not want to absorb the extra costs involved in renting camera, lighting, and sound equipment to conduct screen tests in advance of filming.[2] Andersson had little control over his budget or his own production schedule, leaving a singular artist with the horrible feeling that he'd been forced to release a film that was only two-thirds finished—an experience he vowed never to repeat (Mannberg 1985). "Then he broke from the Swedish film industry in a spectacular way, thought he'd been ganged up on, had conflicts with Svensk Filmindustri, the big giant in Swedish film, and started his own [studio]," said Pia Lundberg, head of the Swedish Film Institute's International Division, in a 2010 interview. "That really got people's attention, buying a building in Stockholm, in Östermalm, and starting his own, completely independent studio with his own little film industry, his own little film world."[3] But Andersson's unprecedented break with the Swedish film industry did not cause him, or his work, to fade from view. When he began making advertising films, he found that he suddenly had free reign to make films the way he wanted, artistically speaking. His clients, who ranged from the Finnish candy company Fazer to the Swedish insurance company Trygg-Hansa to non-Nordic clients such as Air France and Citroën, never concerned themselves with his filmmaking methods and trusted his reputation for high-quality work. "With advertising films, Roy found a clear auteur-style," Gunnar Bergdahl, director of the Gothenburg Film Festival, told Weman in 1998, two years prior to *Songs'* release (Weman 1998, 26). In Sweden, many of these advertisements were screened on large movie theater screens before feature films. Thus countless moviegoers who might have shied away from *Giliap,* or never seen Andersson's award-winning commissioned shorts, were regularly exposed to his distinctive and tragicomic ads featuring antiheroes in ridiculous situations. "Since I was brought up in Sweden during the '80s, Roy Andersson's commercials have affected me way more than any of the movies in film history," Östlund said in an interview posted on the Cannes Film Festival website in conjunction with his 2014 film *Force Majeure* (*Turist*), which won the

Jury Prize in the festival's Un Certain Regard section.[4] As Weman explained in a 1998 article in a Swedish film magazine,

> Roy Andersson has always been there in our collective consciousness. A fantastic film like *A Swedish Love Story* cannot be erased during a lifetime, with *Giliap* he became the suffering artist, and his advertising films have enticed many to laugh in movie theaters. How many other advertising filmmakers do we know by name? There has, in sum, always been a kind of quality brand surrounding Roy Andersson and he has never really had time to disappear (Weman 1998, 29).

The filmmaker's careful cultivation of his brand served him well in the decades leading up to *Songs,* attracting not only paying clients but also talented young film crews and amateur actors who believed they were taking part in high-quality productions. Eva Stenfeldt, a sales clerk at Åhléns department store whom the studio recruited to play the psychologist in the film, said her familiarity with Andersson's commercials was why she agreed to do a screen test for the role. "You don't want to just say yes to anyone. You want to say yes to something that will be good, so that you don't end up in a strange situation," she said in a 2010 interview. (Stenfeldt has also appeared in Andersson's advertising films, for clients including Fazer candy, an English hard rock channel, the newspaper *Aftonbladet*'s special "Kak och bak" (Cake and baking) supplement, the electronics store Elgiganten, and Posten, the Swedish Postal Service.)[5] Yet every time Andersson sought to return to feature filmmaking, he hit a wall. His talent as a filmmaker wasn't at issue. After all, in addition to his celebrated debut film, he had amassed eight Golden Lions for his advertising films at Cannes, Bergman himself had deemed his ad films the best in the world, and his commissioned short films—even one that had been stopped midproduction by the agency that had commissioned it—likewise met with acclaim at domestic and international film festivals. Finding a supportive production studio wasn't at issue, either, as Studio 24 had its own in-house production staff. The biggest obstacle Andersson faced in making *Songs* was finding financial backers willing to allow him to make a feature-length film using the highly unconventional methods he'd honed over the years. This chapter, then, provides a detailed account of the unique filmmaking methods Andersson used to make *Songs* and shows how he succeeded in completing a highly acclaimed film— followed by two films in the same signature style—that contradict our most basic assumptions about filmmaking practices.

Building Up a World

One of the most extraordinary aspects of Studio 24's film practice— and its most costly—is the amount of time and resources spent on building original sets. Every single interior scene in *Songs from the Second Floor* is an environment created in the studio but designed to look like it could be "on location." The Grand Hotel, the furniture store with a street in the background, the bar with the endless traffic jam visible through the windows—all of these and more were built by Studio 24's crew. "A few are ingenious, the kind that make me think, 'Wow!—but how the hell was that scene done?'" Swedish film critic Jan-Olov Andersson wrote in a five-star review in *Aftonbladet* (2000). Even the expansive exterior scenes, such as the sacrifice scene and the final scene at the dump, required major set construction—or, as Studio 24 producer Pernilla Sandström put it, that the crew "redo the entire natural environment"— to create the effects that Andersson wanted. "Roy wants that 100 percent control over the image, the lighting, and everything, which means that you either have to redo the outside, or build inside. And those large indoor sets, they cost a lot," Sandström said.[6] *Songs* was also filmed between 1996 and 2000, before Andersson started using a digital film camera, which meant he had fewer options for manipulating the image postproduction. Every detail had to look right through the camera's lens. To make *Songs*, a film that seeks to crystalize—through grotesque exaggeration—the human condition at the turn of the millennium, Andersson built an entire dystopic world from scratch.

That this was at all feasible was due to Andersson's fully equipped film studio and a dedicated crew. The humiliation Andersson had experienced in making *Giliap*, when his reliance on rented equipment and contracted film crews gave him little control over the production conditions, made him determined to do future operations in-house. In addition to buying camera equipment, Andersson purchased his own lighting, his own props, his own stage makeup, and his own wardrobe of costumes. "Roy doesn't like to rent [things], which has been very smart of him in the long term," said production manager Johan Carlsson, who joined Studio 24 as an intern in the late 1980s and stayed on. Carlsson points out that investing in eighty-two lamps, for example, costs half a million crowns, but then "they've paid for themselves after two years, and you can use them for sixteen more years, totally for free. I think it is very cost effective."[7] The studio's expansive downstairs area, where the sets are built, has a fully equipped workshop, complete with power tools. Upstairs is a kitchen and eating area where the amateur actors and crew were served home-cooked meals on long shooting days—and a piano, in case anyone ever felt like breaking into song. "There was a lot of laughter and a lot of fun," Stenfeldt recalled.[8] The room adjacent to Andersson's office is filled with art books, drafting tables, and wall space for hanging images, a kind of simplified storyboard. This is the room where Andersson would sketch out a scene and discuss it with his crew. Andersson, who had childhood dreams of becoming a painter, "can draw expressfully and well," Carlsson said. According to Carlsson, sometimes his sketches were very basic, but others were really beautiful.[9] Upstairs, above Andersson's office, is an in-house theater; during *Songs*' production, this is where Andersson and his crew would watch the takes from each shoot and determine whether a scene needed to be reshot, which Carlsson said happened with about half of the scenes. Andersson also worked closely with a core crew of about ten people, all of whom were on the studio's payroll and who understood his artistic vision and his methods. The studio had a number of young interns with filmmaking ambitions who'd worked with him on his advertising films, Andersson said, and when it came time to make *Songs*, the studio hired them on full-time. "I think we've hired everyone who came here as [state-sponsored interns]," he said. "I feel proud of that. It feels like we have fulfilled the promise that the system actually contains, but that so many choose only to exploit" (Göransson 2000, 94). Among them was Lisa Alwert, whom the studio ultimately listed as the film's producer because she tended to so many logistical details over the course of filming. Another was Jesper Klevenås, who ended up taking over as the film's cinematographer when István Borbás, who had worked closely with Andersson since 1983 (and who rejoined the crew for *A Pigeon*), had to leave *Songs*' production in 1999 to complete a project he'd previously committed to in his native Hungary.[10]

Klevenås and Borbás said in a joint interview that they believed that the film's elaborately crafted sets helped the inexperienced actors to take their part in the film very seriously. "We almost always work with amateurs, and if you work in a built set, then you can see how much work has gone into it, and it creates a certain respect for the scene," Borbás said. "They see that we're not just playing around, there is a ton of work that goes into this, and then you can require a certain discipline from them, as well."[11] The crew also immersed themselves so completely in the world of the film that it was disorienting to come out of it into the real world, Klevenås said. Many shooting days lasted well into the night, but it was "daytime" inside the studio set where the filming was taking place. "There are big windows with daylight, and then you come out [of the studio] and you're like, 'Wow, it's night!' because it's so damned difficult to reset [your thinking]," Klevenås said. Stenfeldt confirmed that she and other amateur actors were amazed by the efforts that went into building the elaborate sets, a process she got to witness. Because she had a significant speaking part in the scene in a large salon where she questions the girl to be sacrificed in front of society's elders, Stenfeldt came to the studio every day to rehearse in the space while the set was being built, which took several weeks. As a result, Stenfeldt said, she had "very different memories of the film than what you see when it appears on screen." For example, she said, the huge painting on the wall in the background of that scene actually had no head. It didn't need one, since the shot's frame ends just below it, but for the actors, this contributed to the absurdity of the built environment. The "gold frames" of the painting were made of plastic, and the crew pressed Coca-Cola bottles into them to create the indented patterns. "It's so exciting to see how, with such simple materials, they can get it to look so authentic," Stenfeldt said. In the film itself, she said, "it looks like we're on location" rather than on a studio set.[12]

Lana Wachowski (best known for *The Matrix* trilogy she codirected with her brother Andy) has said she was so mesmerized by the aesthetics of the first two films in Andersson's trilogy that in

2012, when she discovered he was at work on the third, she "made a pilgrimage" to Studio 24 in Stockholm to see how he accomplished such visual effects. What astonished Wachowski was not only the painstaking effort that went into building sets for individual scenes—each of them only a few minutes long—but also that Andersson rolled up his sleeves and toiled alongside his crew:

> He builds for three or four weeks, and then he brings in these actors and starts rehearsing—and he's covered in paint because he does a lot of it. And then he's like, "Okay, let's rehearse." Then they shoot in a day. One shot. And he finds this shot. "This is the shot." That's it. They shoot it in a day, and that scene is done. And then he starts building the next set. (J. Smith 2012)

As Andersson's crew attests, there have indeed been times when shooting a single scene was not completed in one day, given that Andersson is notorious for requiring close to fifty takes, including retakes, for a single shot. The scene in *Songs* requiring the most takes, Borbás and Klevenås agreed, was the very first one they shot, which ended up being the tenth tableau in the film: a magician saws a man in half and accidentally injures him. After many takes failed to yield the result Andersson wanted, the director had the crew rebuild the stage floor with the star on it to render a "truer" shade and texture, and he also made some color and style alterations to the audience's costumes—much in the way a painter might add dabs of color and texture on a canvas. Borbás said that the first scene they shot helped them set the tone and aesthetic parameters for the remaining scenes, providing a film that lacks a linear narrative with a striking visual and aesthetic continuity. Carlsson said that Andersson, given his deep interest in painting, likes to paint certain

2.1 Edward Hopper (USA, 1882–1967), *Automat* (1927). Oil on canvas, 71.4 x 91.4 cm. Hopper's depictions of lonely people sitting in New York's bars and restaurants at night provided inspiration for the mood and setting of the film's bar scene in which a son (Stefan Larsson) drinks away the hours while waiting for his father (Lars Nordh). Held at the Des Moines Art Center, which provided the photograph; used with permission.

details of the set himself, such as stone floors or painting patterns on oak or wood furniture and trim. "He also knows a lot about props" and spends much of his time browsing stores for the kinds of tables and chairs he wants, said Carlsson.[13] The precision in Andersson's images, and his attention to minute details, have earned him a reputation as an uncompromising perfectionist. While Carlsson

"The Bar." Screen test 1, take 3, November 4, 1996, at Studio 24. Andersson's filmmaking process always starts with the built environment, and once it starts to take shape, potential actors are brought in for screen tests within that space, during the set's construction. This was the first set the team built for the bar scene, with production manager Johan Carlsson standing in as the bartender and Jesper Klevenås (a crew member who took over for cinematographer István Borbás in 1999) pretending to be a customer. Frame grab.

believes the first half of this label is fitting, he said that "perfectionist" was somewhat inaccurate. "I think that is a misconception about Roy," Carlsson said, while acknowledging that even Andersson has described himself that way. "It's not about having to have things look exactly a certain way. It is about him wanting to sense that he's fundamentally succeeded in what he was striving for. And I think that's two different things."[14] In other words, Andersson could be called an artist who refuses to compromise on his vision for his art, even as he experiments with materials and methods.

2.3 "The Bar 2." Screen test 2, November 16, 1997, at LännaAteljéerna Studio, where Andersson's team built a new, expanded set that could accommodate the traffic jam outside the windows. Roy Andersson stands in as the bartender, and his longtime colleague Kalle Boman, the film producer who has owned LännaAteljéerna since 1971, stands in as the father. Frame grab.

In conventional film production, you start with a script, cast the actors, spend weeks on preproduction details involving the film's locations, then hire local film teams to assist with set details. In contrast, every scene in *Songs* began with set design and building, because the world of the film is critical to Andersson's aesthetic. Indeed, Carlsson has estimated that building sets constitutes 90 percent of what goes on in the studio (Oscarsson 2103). In his unsuccessful funding proposals to the Swedish Film Institute in the early 1990s, in place of a script, Andersson described the created spaces where the individual scenes are set. "The environments are archetypical. The

2.4 "The Bar 2." Completed shot in November 1997 at LännaAteljéerna Studio. The bartender (Inger Christell-Malmberg) tells the sooty father, Kalle (Lars Nordh), that his son Stefan (Stefan Larsson), slumped over a beer in the background, has been waiting for him for hours. Photo courtesy of Studio 24; used with permission.

foundational mood is Europe with its cultural and historical background."[15] Alwert said that during the early stages of filming, certain scenes proved too large or complex to film in the space Studio 24 had at that time, so they were forced to build certain sets in other local studio spaces. One of these was the bar scene, in which Andersson wanted to achieve the kind of pensive alienation that infuses American painter Edward Hopper's (1882–1967) images of lonely figures in New York's bars and restaurants (e.g., figure 2.1). Building the kind of wide angle and deep background that the endless traffic jam in the background required proved impossible at Studio 24 (see figure 2.2), so the set was rebuilt and ultimately filmed in LännaAteljéerna studio, a space owned by Andersson's longtime colleague Kalle Boman (figure 2.2). Studio 24 also rented a space at Storängsbotten Studio, which had previously housed a television station, for six months to build sets and film the burned-out furniture store and the airport departure terminal scenes. The furniture store set was rebuilt three times, Alwert said. After that, the crew started looking around for ways to expand Studio 24's own space so that they would no longer have to rent studio space from others. About a year into filming, Alwert discovered that the building next door that had housed a Svensk Filmindustri (SF) movie theater known as "Puck" from 1934 to 1982 stood empty. "I said to [Andersson], 'I think it's empty back there—shouldn't we make a hole in the wall?'" She laughed at the memory. "And that's what happened. It was quite crucial that we got access to that space."[16] The first set they built there, she recalled, was the asylum corridor scene, "The Dumb Brother—The Corridor," shot in January 1999 (see figure 3.1).

A particular challenge that arose in making *Songs* was that Studio 24 had never housed a full-scale feature film production, which required updates to the facilities, Alwert recalled. Even after production began, the crew was continuously renovating and reorganizing the studio to meet various needs that emerged during filming. These ranged from major tasks, such as building a new costume storage space in the cellar, to more trivial ones, such as labeling all of the blazers so that they would know which blazer to put on which actor in scenes that involved a lot of extras. At that time, Studio 24 had no office staff to speak of, Carlsson said, and no finance division. Everyone who worked there was involved in production—many of them filling multiple roles, such as costume design and set building. There was no telephone switchboard, and the entire crew shared a single mobile phone that they had to take turns bringing with them on errands, which sometimes sparked irritation, Alwert recalled.

"We were a fairly inexperienced crew," she said. "There were a few who had worked with [Andersson], but this was something totally different from doing advertising films. So I think much of our efforts went toward trying to find a tone, feel your way forward."[17] This also sometimes resulted in conflicts among crewmembers. Carlsson, one of the original crew, even left the production for a time, returning to assist with the film's final scenes (and then staying on for the next two films in the trilogy).[18]

Andersson's crew quickly found that there were particular challenges involved in filming the large outdoor scenes on the Swedish coastal islands of Gotland (see figure 3.3) and Öland (see figure 4.4), located about 130 miles (211 kilometers) and 270 miles (432 kilometers) south of Stockholm, respectively. There were, of course, the logistical challenges of making extensive modifications to the natural landscape, but those were resolved with the help of friendly locals. In the sacrifice scene on Gotland, for example, there were windmills on the horizon, which Andersson didn't want in the shot (see figure 3.3). They could not remove the windmills, but they were able to hide them behind the large pole that rises up in the middle of the shot so that they can't be seen in the camera's frame. Stenfeldt recounted that they set up the camera at the angle they needed, then had the owner turn off the windmills just at the right moment so they would remain hidden behind the pole. "It wouldn't have worked if they hadn't been so cooperative," Alwert said, recalling that the people who owned the limestone quarry where the shot took place wanted no compensation. "They thought it was kind of fun" she said. "They thought, 'This is kind of good for Slite [the tiny town where the shoot took place]. Something is happening!'" Andersson said the landowners even helped out with the shoot by building up the ground under the cliff, so that the young gymnast (Helene Mathiasson) who was hired to play Anna in the scene would not have to fall as far when she was pushed off the cliff. In thanks, Andersson gave them a copy of a humanist anthology Studio 24 had produced, *Successful Freezing of Mr. Moro* (*Lyckad nedfrysning av Herr Moro*, 1992).[19] The sacrifice scene on Gotland was being prepared at the same time as the train station scene was being filmed in the Stockholm suburb of Täby, Alwert recalled. This meant that a young and inexperienced team was juggling the logistics of two major scenes at two far-flung locations at once, which caused tension. Klevenås recalled that everyone was so exhausted by the time they'd finished these shoots, in autumn 1998, that the crew took vacation time (Swedish law mandates five weeks of paid vacation a year). No one had expected the film's production schedule to stretch out so long; in fact, Studio 24 had even printed business cards that listed the production years as 1996–98, Klevenås said. "We had worked so hard for an entire year," he said. "So we decided, we are taking a break. I think it was really stressful for Roy.... This was his 'comeback,' so when nothing was happening, he found that really tough, to take a break. But it was necessary."[20]

The major outdoor scenes on Gotland ("The Sacrifice") and on Öland ("The Thousand Dead") were each shot in October, one year apart. The weather—uncharacteristically sunny for southern Sweden in October—nearly foiled each shoot, Borbás said. Lighting is critically important for Andersson's film aesthetics: he constructs evenly lit sets in which all elements are equally exposed so that that there are "no shadows to hide in," as he put it in an American national radio interview in June 2015 (Ulaby). Soft lighting is also necessary to maintain the optical illusions, Borbás and Klevenås explained; if the sun shone too brightly, one could tell that the crowd figures in the deepest background of the sacrifice scene were actually made of masonite, spoiling the illusion of a crowd extending endlessly to the horizon in a scene that already employed a thousand extras. In the film's culminating outdoor scene, on Öland, the model city the crew built on the empty horizon needed diffuse light to appear authentic. After spending more than a month to build each outdoor set, the crew was forced to wait for the right kind of natural light to show up—and then pray for it to hold while they summoned the army of extras and crew members required to complete each shot. The crew, accustomed to taking fifty or more takes, had to make do with four to six takes for the outdoor shots, because they could film only when the lighting was ideal. For each shoot, the crew had to wait an extra week once the set was ready for the right weather and lighting conditions. In a joint interview in 2010, Borbás and Klevenås described how this worked when they shot the film's final scene on the limestone plain on Öland:

Borbás: It felt like in Savannah, it was so warm, and we thought that maybe it would never get cloudy. So [Andersson] talked to the farmers in the area and asked, "What's up with the weather?" and they said, "If clouds come, they might stay for two days, and after that anything can happen, because then it will be autumn, and then it changes every day." And then on Friday, the clouds came, and at two o'clock the light was really beautiful. So we decided to film on Saturday. It was a little tough to gather together all of the extras—it would have been better on Sunday. But we were determined—"No, we have to do it tomorrow"—because the farmers said it would hold for two days at most. And the next day when we awoke, it was sunny again— "Damn it, how is this going to work?" But then suddenly at one o'clock it began to get windy, and then the perfect light came and the perfect wind.

Klevenås: Yeah, really, it was so dramatic, the wind filled his coat, and—

Borbás: It was actually a remarkable experience. It was pretty pleas-ant for the extras to rehearse, because it was quite warm in the late morning, and then the perfect light came, and we took six takes. It was extremely complicated to put back all of the extras [who had to jump up out of the earth as the risen dead] in the ground and do another take.[21]

By the fourth take, Andersson and Borbás were pleased with the result; nonetheless, they urged the extras and the crew to hold out for two more takes. At the end of a long day of filming, the crew collapsed, exhausted, into bed, thinking they might continue with a few more takes the next day, just to make sure. But that night, a wind storm leveled the set, littering the limestone plain with set materials and with the ample tents filled with costumes, makeup, and other equipment, and turning an already complex set breakdown into a massive cleanup operation. Andersson soured on outdoor location shoots after that, Borbás said. Every scene of the subsequent two films in Andersson's trilogy—including those that appear to be outdoors, and even one that involved twenty-five horses—were shot in the studio.

Money, Money, Money

There were a number of breaks in production over the four years it took to finish the film, and most of the time, it was because Studio 24 had run out of money. Whenever this happened, they were forced to set aside the feature film production and make another advertising film or two so that they could continue. Sandström, Studio 24's in-house producer, didn't join Andersson's team until 1998, when *Songs'* filming had already been under way for two years. She came on board as production secretary, not formally taking over managing the finances until the second film in the trilogy, *You, the Living* (Cloarec 2008). For a while, there was a crew member tasked with managing the finances, Alwert said, but then he left the studio, and for a time it fell to Alwert to make sure there was enough money on hand to pay everyone's salaries—by far the largest part of the studio's budget. As Sandström later pointed out, Studio 24 needs to pay the salaries of everyone who paints and builds sets for weeks and months at a time. Another expense, Sandström said, was that Andersson would shoot daily test shots on thirty-five-millimeter film of each scene as it developed. Most directors just take a video test to make sure a scene looks right, Sandström said, but it was important for Andersson to see what the scenes looked like on the big screen. "It's mostly to make sure that these perspective-paintings work, that they do fool the eye, so that you can see immediately on the screen the next day, 'Does this work on screen? Can you see the lie, or do we need to make some changes?'" she said in an interview.[22]

Andersson's unconventional filmmaking methods are by far the biggest obstacle for securing funding, Sandström said, because it is difficult to explain his vision and his methods in words rather than images. All of Andersson's efforts to describe the film in words to the Swedish Film Institute failed utterly; officials couldn't make any sense of his written proposals and rejected them all (Göransson 2000, 26–27). These attempts, on file in the Swedish Film Institute (SFI) library, contain philosophical overviews and descriptions of the proposed film's environments and scenarios, but no dialogue, which typically comprises the bulk of any film script. One of the proposals even acknowledges that a script was expected but declines to provide one: "The manuscript for the film project *Songs from the Second Floor* is in progress and is expected to be ready in mid-December 1993. Here follows a little material that can give a certain indication of content and tone." The proposal continues, "This film project will raise for discussion many essential existential questions. Most of them have always occupied the human being. Some have particular relevance for our time."[23] Frustrated by SFI's refusals, Andersson took on more advertising work. In 1995, the studio produced thirteen major commercials. By the end of that year, Andersson had made enough money to self-finance a portion of the film that could be used to show to funding agencies. "I could choose between buying a sailboat or start filming," he said in 2000. "I chose to film" (Göransson 2000, 28). Andersson used his own money to shoot the film's first fifteen minutes, including the subway scene (see cover photo) and the bar scene (figure 2.4). By 1997, when Andersson was ready to show his sample clip to SFI, the institute had implemented a film commissioner (*filmkonsulent*) system for judging the merits of funding proposals.[24] Film commissioner Mats Arehn, who had long been familiar with Andersson's work, watched the clip and immediately granted him eight million Swedish crowns (just short of one million dollars)—nearly twice the funding level of the average Swedish film.[25] To apply for SFI funding, Studio 24 had had to have a domestic distributor lined up. Studio 24 chose Triangelfilm in Malmö in large part because it was the only distributor who offered to pay an advance sum for distribution rights. Studio 24 also received money from advance distribution sales in Germany, France, Norway, and Denmark (Tapper 2002, 72).

Songs was a historically expensive film by Swedish standards. While its final price tag of fifty million Swedish crowns (roughly 5.5 million dollars at May 2000 exchange rates) is similar to that of many independent American films, such a sum was unprecedented in Swedish cinema. At the start of filming, however, it was unclear exactly how much the film would cost. There was no set budget, Alwert said; rather, they just worked from scene to scene. The larger, most expensive scenes cost up to one million crowns each, and by 1998, they were running out of money, even after Studio 24 had invested more than twenty million crowns of its own resources, in cash and kind, in the film.[26] Andersson and Alwert traveled to the Gothenburg Film Festival to show clips to potential funders. Before leaving for the festival, they found out that the room at the festival where they were to show the film didn't have a thirty-five-millimeter film projector, so they had to haul one with them on the train, Alwert said. Ultimately, they managed to secure funding from media companies all over the Nordic region: Nordisk Film & TV Fond, the Danish Film Institute, Danmarks Radio, Sveriges Television, Norsk Rikskringkasting, and Finsk TV. Still, with a few critical scenes left, they were once again running out of cash. "I think there is an erroneous picture that people here in Sweden have, that Roy has made all of these advertising films and he has twenty million crowns in a bank in Switzerland," Carlsson said. "But that's not how it is." Whatever income he has, he invests in his films and in the studio. "There are seldom piles of money lying around," Carlsson said.[27] In fact, Andersson once famously sued both SFI and the Gothenburg Film Festival to recoup some of the cost overruns on his short film *World of Glory* (1991), which ended up costing 2 million crowns more than the 1.7 million crowns he'd been allotted for the commissioned nine-minute film—which ended up being fourteen minutes long. Andersson sought in vain to argue that "the film was 'nine minutes long, artistic time'"; however, SFI and Studio 24 eventually settled out of court (Göransson 2000, 89–90). Decades later, even after the success of his trilogy, Andersson told a film reporter, "For a long time I've actually had to take loans so I have many debts!" (Evry 2015).

Coproducer Philippe Bober of the Copenhagen-based Co-Production Office, which was to handle the film's foreign distribution deals, helped Studio 24 make contact with a number of European cultural funds, most significantly ARTE (Association Relative à la Télévision Européenne), a Franco-German TV network; Canal+, a French premium cable television channel; and ZDF (Zweites Deutsches Fernsehen), a public German TV network. Even with Bober to make the contacts, however, it wasn't simple to make a case for such an unconventional film made by a filmmaker who had taken twenty-five years off from feature filmmaking. "He doesn't write a traditional film script that you can send in and apply for funding and talk with people about," Sandström said. "He has to get the funders to trust that this is going to happen, with only a few images and Roy's explanation to trust that it will be something good, something he says it is going to be, without being able to prove it on paper." Some funding sources even require filmmakers to sign a contract stating that the film will be made exactly as appears in the manuscript, Sandström said. "You have to convince these financial backers and coproducers that they cannot get involved at all, but at the same time, they should give you a lot of money. That's what is tricky."[28] ARTE did want to see a film script before they would consider funding the film, so Andersson wrote one—three years and four months into filming—that consisted mostly of the dialogue that had emerged organically through the filming process. But the studio also set up a meeting with ARTE's representatives at the Berlin Film Festival and arranged to show them a clip. After they saw it, they signed on immediately, as did Canal+, said Andersson in an interview.[29] Securing such diverse sources of financial backing not only helped Studio 24 complete *Songs from the Second Floor*; it also established partnerships between the studio and these networks that continued with the remaining films in Andersson's trilogy.

Following its spectacular win at the Cannes Film Festival in May 2000, *Songs from the Second Floor* premiered at the Swedish box office on October 6, 2000, in twenty-one copies that circulated all over the country. Most Swedish films are in theaters for less than six months, Sandström said, and normally as ticket sales begin to taper off, studios release the films on DVD. But this was not the case with *Songs*, which showed consistent numbers at the box office for up to a year following its release, making the studio wonder how they should time the release of the DVD. According to SFI statistics, 90,430 movie theater tickets to *Songs* were sold in 2000, the year of its premiere, and an additional 70,900 movie theater tickets sold during the remainder of its run. (Comparatively speaking, Liv Ullmann's acclaimed art film *Faithless* (*Trolösa*), which was scripted by Bergman, sold 66,582 tickets during 2000 and 3,345 afterward, and Lukas Moodysson's feel-good film *Together* (*Tillsammans*)—by far the most popular film of the year in Sweden—garnered 849,134 tickets sold in 2000 and another 33,209 thereafter.) After *Songs* swept the Swedish film awards the following January, Andersson knew he wouldn't have trouble securing SFI funding for the next film in his trilogy, which would be *You, the Living* (*Du Levande*, 2007). *Songs* effectively ended Andersson's long estrangement from Sweden's major film institutions.

Despite international critical acclaim, however, the film performed less well than expected at box offices abroad, and in two major European markets, France and Germany, distribution problems were to blame. "Andersson's film had to wait nearly two years in Germany, until a distribution deal finally brought it into cinemas," Reinhold Zwick, a German scholar, later wrote. "Given its bleak humor, this gloomy film was predicted to die at the box office. And so it did" (Zwick 2008, 99). In France, a financial dispute between Bober and the local distributor caused the distributor to withdraw the film from the French market entirely for five years, until the distributor's contract ran out. At that point, the Franco-German television network ARTE, which had helped fund the film's completion, helped Studio 24 release the film in France on DVD, Sandström said.[30]

An Archive of Characters

Conventional wisdom has it that a great film requires great actors, which—one may assume—should be professionally trained. When Studio 24 put out a casting call in 1996 for a role in Roy Andersson's comeback film, hundreds of young men flocked to the studio to audition for the role of the poet who would read lines from César Vallejo's poem "Stumble between Two Stars," the film's chief inspiration (as I discuss in the next chapter).[31] The studio screen-tested hundreds of people, including, but not limited to, professionally trained actors (see figure 2.3). Among those who auditioned for the role, Alwert said, were actors who have since become famous, including Mikael Persbrandt (known for Susanne Bier's Oscar-winning film *In a Better World/Hævnen*, 2010; as well as Peter Jackson's *Hobbit* films, 2013–14); Shanti Roney (whose breakout role was in Moodysson's *Together* in 2000, and since 2012 has played detective Paul Hjelm in a TV miniseries scripted by Swedish crime fiction writer Arne Dahl); Tobias Aspelin (known for *The New Man/Den nya människan*, 2007, directed by Klaus Härö; and *Love and Happiness/Krama mig*, directed by Kristina Humle, 2005); and troubadour Stefan Sundström (known for *Expectations/ Svenska hjältar*, directed by Daniel Bergman, 1997; and the TV series *Eva & Adam*, 1999–2000). At the same time, members of the crew fanned out across Stockholm, looking for ordinary people that seemed like the characters they were trying to cast, which was their tried-and-true method for casting advertising films. "After a while, you learn how to approach people without scaring them," Alwert said. Then one night, Andersson and Alwert were staking out hot spots in the Stockholm neighborhood of Södermalm where young men typically hang out, and at the restaurant Pelikan, Larsson was sitting at the next table with two friends, acting "very expressive," as Larsson said later with a smile. Alwert approached him and asked him if he'd like to audition for a role in Andersson's new film. "'Of course!' I said after having had a few beers," Larsson said. "But my expectations were low. I thought, that would be fun to try."[32] As the months dragged on, Larsson was called in for repeated interviews and screen tests, where he read opposite young women who were presumably meant to play a girlfriend role. Eventually, the team was frustrated in its efforts to find the right poet and realized that the best solution was to have a mute, tortured poet whose poetry was recited to him by a sensitive and troubled younger brother. Larsson was cast in the brother's role, and most of the other roles in the film went to amateur actors as well. Only one professional actor was cast: Bengt C. W. Carlsson, best known at the time for this work in theater, who played the capitalist boss Lennart in the film—a role that showed only his feet in the film's opening scene.[33] Andersson said Carlsson's voice was perfect for playing the "Oracle in a Solarium," as the scene was titled.

Casting amateur actors was by then a tried-and-true method for Andersson, who had found some of his most delightful antiheroes for advertising films while shopping or gassing up the car. "I spend a lot of time going out and finding characters," he said. "What matters is to find people with presence [närvaro], who are authentic in their movements and in their dialogue, that are interesting to look at." His crew has searched among trained actors as well, "but the Swedish acting corps is frightfully small compared with the general Swedish population," Andersson said, "so it is hardly strange that we did not find what we were looking for there, but rather in other places" (Göransson 2000, 69–70). Before filming began, he already had amassed sixteen hundred "characters" in his database (with each entry consisting of contact information and clothing and shoe size) through his advertising film work and short films. One of these characters was Nordh, whom the studio had recruited earlier to play a stingy dairy farmer from Småland (the same rural southern province that IKEA founder Ingvar Kamprad is from) in a series of eight advertising films for the Finnish branch of the dairy company Arla. Production manager Jens Munter had found Nordh while he was shopping at IKEA's Kungens Kurva store on the outskirts of Stockholm and urged him to come in for a screen test. Nordh, who was from Småland, had retained his provincial dialect even after moving to Stockholm and spending many years working in the print shop of a local tabloid newspaper. Nordh's "presence" in the commercials made such an impression on Finnish viewers that he became a celebrity in Finland, and Arla had him pose for a special calendar featuring him in monthly photos with various Finnish pop celebrities. The Arla films also netted Nordh the Nordic acting prize for best actor in an ad film, a distinction won the previous year by the legendary Swedish actor Ernst-Hugo Järegård (Göransson 2000, 69). During *Songs*' four-year production, the studio added another four hundred characters to its database. One of these was Stenfeldt, whom Alwert approached when she was working in the hosiery section at Åhléns department store at Karlaplan. Alwert took out her camera and filmed her right there, Stenfeldt recalls, then she later got called in for an actual screen test. Stenfeldt's distinctive voice, which was decisive in her casting, has caused a number of the regular customers in the store to recognize her from the film. Larsson, who had one of the largest speaking roles in the film, said that after the film came out "it often happened that people would recognize me, but they couldn't place me. They would say, 'Where do you work? Do we work at the same place?' And I'd say, 'No . . . ,'" Larsson said.[34]

The Swedish word Andersson and his crew use to describe the amateur actors is *statist*, which usually denotes a nonspeaking role—an "extra" in Hollywood film parlance. But true to his trivialist vision of elevating the lowly, "extras" take center stage in *Songs from the Second Floor*, with quite a few of them becoming, paradoxically enough, *talstatister* (speaking extras). "We were all extras—even me," said Nordh. "That's why everyone is white[-faced]. Everyone is equal." This ethos extended to how the filmmaker treated his actors and crew, Nordh said in 2000. "He is honest and good-hearted. He treats all people alike," Nordh explained. "He has a special talent and you cannot deny him anything. He can get you to do anything" (Lagher 2000, 26). This talent came in handy during grueling shooting days, which began at 9 a.m. for those with speaking parts and often ended at 1 a.m. Most of the amateur actors had other jobs, although a few were retired. This meant that after a long workweek, they would come to the studio on Saturday or Sunday—sometimes both—and work on the film scenes. Larsson said it was difficult for him and Nordh, the only amateur actors who were part of the production from start to finish, to go on vacation or make plans during those four years. Larsson recounted one humorous moment when Nordh had had enough. "There was take after take after take, and we'd have to have our makeup touched up, and finally he just freaked out and said, 'Roy! You like to make films! I like to be a coach potato!' and stormed off. Roy ran after him—'Lasse! Lasse!'" Larsson chuckled.[35] Nordh, for his part, remembers very clearly the exhaustion he felt. Nordh worked nights as a printer at the daily newspaper *Aftonbladet,* and sometimes he would get calls from Andersson in the middle of the night asking him if he could come to the studio. Still, Nordh, a proud union member, respected not only Andersson's artistic talent but also the honest way he treated all of those who worked for him. Studio 24 strictly follows the guidelines of Teaterförbundet (Theater Guild) in paying its amateur actors, and everyone interviewed for this book said they were well paid for their work. The studio also sought to keep the cast's and crew's spirits up with home-cooked food, regular coffee breaks (as is standard in Swedish workplaces), and shared bottles of wine later in the evening. Once, Nordh said, the studio's cook asked him what his favorite meal was, and he answered "paltbröd med fläsk"—a traditional Swedish country meal that consists of bread baked in blood, then dried, and served with grilled pork and sometimes onion—something one is not likely to find in cosmopolitan Stockholm. "So she made it for me and she put a note on it that said, 'Lasse's—no one can touch this!'" Nordh recalled. "They were incredible people who were there."[36]

Acting in Andersson's films did not come naturally for the cast, even though they'd been cast precisely because they seemed natural and authentic in their particular roles. Once they were in front of the camera, they had to learn to relax, to carry themselves and speak their lines in a "natural" way. One benefit to doing so many takes, Larsson and Stenfeldt both said, was that at some point, they felt so exhausted that they couldn't act anymore, and then all of their dialogue and gestures began to come more naturally. "It's very difficult acting, actually, because he has taken away all mannerisms, and that's a way to bring out the child in a person," Larsson said. "The adults become children, and I think it's extremely hard. I'm supposed to be obvious, but not."[37] Andersson has said that "body language is many times at least as important as the dialogue, and the pauses are more important than the words. In the same way, the one who listens can be more interesting than the one who speaks" (Grönkvist 2000, 19). These elements came to bear in the scene that Larsson found to be by far his most difficult: the taxi scene. It is a deep and multilayered shot. In the far background, the taxi is surrounded by a street-level view of a traffic jam, complete with commuters waiting in vain at bus stops and the flagellants from the furniture store scene appearing in the frame midway through the shot. A tipsy, nervous colonel gets into the back seat of the taxi and prattles on about the country's traditions. In the very foreground of the scene sits Stefan in the film's closest shot; his face is right in front of the camera, as if the lens were positioned directly behind the rear view mirror. Larsson's challenge was to create a presence that was mildly irritated but polite, and one that didn't overshadow the complex layers of action happening behind him, both inside and outside of the taxi. It took what seemed to him an endless number of takes to get it right. "You begin to sense it yourself when it began to come to life, then Roy began to roar with laughter, " Larsson said. "And for me that was incredibly comforting, to hear that laugh that I've never heard anything like."[38] Andersson's laughter would grow in proportion to how well the scene was going, the actors said. "He sits there and laughs at his own lines of dialogue no matter how many times he's heard them," Nordh said in 2000. "Sometimes he had to leave because he laughed so hard during the fiftieth take" (Lahger 2000, 26).

The levity and camaraderie that characterized the set between takes were important, the amateur actors said, because Andersson's slow, meticulous, and ever-evolving production process demanded a great deal of endurance, patience, and flexibility from both actors and crew. After *Songs* was done, Nordh agreed to play a supporting role in a more conventional film: *Sidetracked/Villospår* (directed by Leif Magnusson, 2001), a Henning Mankell murder mystery starring Rolf Lassgård as Detective Wallander, just to see how it compared to an Andersson production. Nordh was stunned by the frenetic pace of conventional film production in Sweden, in which three to four scenes had to be shot in a single day, with far fewer retakes.[39] Andersson, on the other hand, would fine-tune a scene until it "felt right," which could take weeks. Nordh said that while the amateur actors typically would receive their lines a couple of weeks ahead of time so that they could learn them, Andersson would often change them after a few rehearsals or even between takes. Andersson acknowledges that he sometimes modifies his films' dialogue on the spot to better suit the environment or the amateur actor who would be speaking the lines. In effect, the script emerges as the set and the characters' "presence" emerge. Nordh, who appears in many of the film's scenes and struggled to learn his lines, was frustrated by this process. "You can never get him to change a text, not even a comma. Then he changes it himself as much as he likes. If you'd already learned a whole page by heart, you could get a little fretful," he said in a 2000 interview (Lahger 2000, 26). Larsson took recorder lessons for weeks to prepare for the scene in the kitchen where Stefan and his girlfriend play a song on the recorder together. Then one week before the scene was to be shot, Andersson decided on a different song. Larsson, a computer engineer who had never played a recorder before, found it impossible to learn a new piece of music in a week's time, so Andersson made plans to dub it instead. Ultimately, Benny Andersson's musical score is what we hear during that scene, which seemed to him the perfect interlude of light and hope for the score's recurring melody to be played on the recorder. (This scene is one of several instances of nondiegetic sound that, visually speaking, appears to be diegetic, as I discuss in chapter 3.) Stenfeldt, who appeared in two of the film's darkest scenes—the sacrifice and the Grand Hotel—said the jovial mood on the set made it possible for her and others to relax during breaks and take things seriously once filming began. This despite the fact that during repeated takes of the Grand Hotel scene she would get splashed with fake vomit made of fruit soup, foam rubber, and shampoo. Often she had to wash her hair, change clothes, and reapply makeup between scenes. When it came to the sacrifice scene, she said, the crew made a point of asking everyone ahead of time whether they minded acting in a scene in which a child gets pushed off a cliff. No one objected, Stenfeldt said, and seeing the set constructed in front of their eyes lessened the scene's impact for those acting in it. "When it went bit by bit like that in front of you, when you see all the scenery, how they build everything up, when they made that foam rubber ramp that the girl fell into, there was no feeling that it was horrible," Stenfeldt said. "It is when you first see the film that you think, 'What have I done?'"[40]

3

Intermediality: Film, Poetry, Painting, Music

From its earliest stages, *Songs from the Second Floor* was inspired by great writers and great artists whose work Andersson admired. In an early project description dated September 1994, Andersson writes, "The film is held together by a man who reads a poem. And that poem takes us on an enormous journey."[1] Another draft of the description, hand-dated November 1994, titles the film "Songs from the Second Floor (An Existential Comedy)" and begins with the following epigraph:

> Our life is a journey
> Through winter and night
> We look for our way
> In a sky without light.
> (Song of the Swiss Guards 1793)[2]

In these drafts, Andersson, who studied literature at Lund University and dreamed of becoming an author or a painter before he was accepted to film school, evokes two of his literary heroes: the Peruvian modernist poet César Vallejo and the French satirist Louis-Ferdinand Céline. The epigraph above also opens Céline's 1932 novel *Journey to the End of the Night* (*Voyage au bout de la nuit*), which Andersson calls "literary history's most interesting novel" (and whose mark on the film will be discussed in the next chapter).[3] The finished film would reference both Céline's and Vallejo's writings, alongside a motley array of other literary allusions, such as Swedish playwright August Strindberg's pioneering expressionist work *A Dream Play* (*Ett drömspel*, 1901), the Biblical Old Testament book of Ecclesiastes, and, of course, Beckett's *Waiting for Godot*. While Andersson is hardly the first filmmaker to incorporate literature or Scripture into his script, the ways in which he weaves them together with other artistic allusions—namely, from painting and music—into his own distinctive film language goes beyond mere sampling. Rather, Andersson sees them as essential ingredients in a new kind of film language that achieves its full potential through intermediality.

Chiel Kattenbelt has helpfully defined intermediality as mutual influence, or "co-relations between different media that result in a redefinition of the media that are influencing each other, which in turn leads to a refreshed perception" (2008, 25). While the intermediality of film and theater have been fairly well studied, literature and painting have long been regarded primarily as source material for adaptation rather than being constitutive of the language of film.[4] By creating films that function as "three-dimensional paintings," as Jesper Klevenås put it, and emulating Beckettian dialogue in scenes that require Chaplinesque comic timing, Andersson seeks to unlock the film medium's unexplored potential.[5] As Andersson wrote in a letter to the Swedish Film Institute in 1993, the art of film "possesses a potential with regard to philosophical clarity, philosophical gravity, and philosophical engagement that is much greater than what we believe it capable of. Here I am referring to the visual, filmic, potential, not so much the [written] word."⁶ Indeed, aside from a dedication to Vallejo in the film's opening frame, *Songs* does not name any of the great writers whose work Andersson evokes through the dialogue. In the world of the film, the characters that speak the appropriated lines do not identify their sources, and there are no cues to indicate that they might be switching from actual dialogue to reciting from literature or Scripture, blurring the boundaries between literary, religious, and everyday speech. There is also no attempt to render the citations faithfully; Andersson's script freely modifies citations of verse and Scripture, including having a character cite extensively from one of Vallejo's poems in truncated form, out of order, and across several scenes. At first, these imprecise quotations might seem to trivialize the canonical works from which they come. However, in the world of the film, any number of ordinary people are invoking these phrases from memory in response to everyday life situations—in some cases, perhaps, without knowing exactly where the words came from. After all, in a society like Sweden's, possessing a cultural canon, universal education, and a high literacy rate, there are going to be some common frames of reference, and such ubiquitous evocations in everyday life situations testify to the enduring relevance of the humanities.⁷ The fact that the characters do not recall the quoted works perfectly arguably gives them an air of authenticity. Thus, paradoxically, while these fragmented lines are recognizable as literary and Scriptural references, Andersson empties them of their literariness and instead makes them integral components of "trivialist" human moments he renders cinematically.

A similar process is at work in Andersson's abundant appropriations of art historical images in *Songs*. In addition to Jacques Callot and Edward Hopper, the film's scenes have been inspired by art works by Pieter Bruegel the Elder (the Netherlands, 1525–1569), Otto Dix (Germany, 1891–1969), Francisco Goya (Spain, 1746–1828),

Hugo Simberg (Finland, 1873–1917), Nils Dardel (Sweden, 1888–1943), Honoré Daumier (France, 1808–1879), Vilhelm Hammershøi (Denmark, 1869–1916), and Ilya Repin (Russia, 1844–1930), among others. But rather than faithfully render the artists' paintings on film, Andersson has allowed these images—many of which he had pondered for decades leading up to *Songs*—to inform and inspire the settings for his film. They, too, have been emptied of specific times, places, or authorial signatures, but the images' essences—the grand, and sometimes absurd, questions about humanity that they have provoked Andersson to ponder—take filmic form in *Songs*. In a sense, the film's fusion of art, literature, and philosophy that present common existential questions echoes an earlier project of which Andersson is quite proud: *Successful Freezing of Mr. Moro*, a 1992 collection of famous humanist writings from Vallejo to Simone de Beauvoir paired with iconic photographs, which Andersson coedited with Kalle Boman and István Borbás at the behest of the Stockholm City Council in an attempt to encourage more high school students to pursue social service vocations (as I discuss in the next chapter). Unlike this book, however, *Songs* does not keep the words and images separate but associated; rather, he blends everything together to create an abstract, intermedial language that he asserts is first and foremost cinematic. (The decision by New York's Museum of Modern Art to hold a 2009 retrospective in Andersson's honor arguably bolsters the intermedial claims of the director's *œuvre*.)[8] All of Andersson's work, from his writings to his films, is predicated on two conjoined assumptions: the intrinsic value of human life, and the critical role of the arts in perpetuating this value.

Given Andersson's passion for poetry, painting, and music (he plays trombone, is a jazz aficionado, and during the filming of *Songs* kept a 1964 white Fender Stratocaster electric guitar plugged in near his desk to cut loose from time to time[9]), it might be tempting to read his films as either pastiches of, or homages to, the great artists he most admires. (One might even add sculpture to his list of fine arts, as Studio 24 also put its considerable set design skills in service of the *Sweden and the Holocaust* living history exhibit at the Forum for Living History in Stockholm in 2007.) However, art appreciation per se is not part of Andersson's filmmaking method; rather, once the work of another master enters Andersson's film world, it undeniably serves Andersson's vision rather than its original creator's. The particular intermediality that forms the basis of Andersson's film language thus goes beyond the imitation of "the hallowed arts" that André Bazin argues has been the practice of filmmakers since the medium's origins.[10] Indeed, Bazin's writings on painting and cinema, theater and cinema, and "mixed cinema" treat the interart correspondences of these various art forms while keeping their medial essences intact, asserting that the main virtue of such appropriations is one art form's ability to foster knowledge and appreciation of another. In "Painting and Cinema," for example, Bazin writes that "there can be virtually no appreciation or aesthetic enjoyment of a painting without some form of prior initiation, without some form of pictorial education that allows the spectator to make that effort of abstraction as a result of which he can clearly distinguish between the mode of existence of the painted surface and of the world around him."[11] While *Songs* might well inspire cinephiles to explore the work of the great masters whose work Andersson calls upon to craft his stunning images, the purpose of this chapter is not to create an inventory of the filmmaker's artistic appropriations. Rather, it is to examine the striking intermediality that infuses, and even structures, Andersson's unique film language. In Andersson's view, the best films are those that draw from a rich humanist tradition that predates cinema by hundreds of years, yet exploit the communicative powers of cinema and its unprecedented access to human sensibilities in the twenty-first century. Half a century after Frankfurt School theorists dismissed cinema as an anti-intellectualist instrument of mass culture, Andersson has joined that legion of intellectuals—Vallejo among them—who have asserted that the language of cinema harbors a unique potential to restore critical consciousness to public life.[12]

Film and Poetry

The writers whose work Andersson samples the most clearly in *Songs*—Vallejo, Céline, Strindberg, and Beckett—have much in common with one another and, unsurprisingly, with their appropriator. While only one is a Frenchman, all of them lived and wrote in Paris at some point in their lives. (Andersson has not lived in Paris, but the French film industry has been very important to his rise as an auteur, in terms of funding and awards and recognition.) All of the writers were considered intellectual radicals or avant-gardists but remained fiercely independent and did not affiliate with a movement. All of them railed against the bourgeoisie, offended cultural authorities, and identified with the working class. And all of them ultimately concluded that the roots of all good and evil were to be found here on earth rather than in the cosmos.

Andersson has said he first encountered Vallejo's poetry in 1975, when he read Marianne Sandels and Pierre Zekeli's Swedish translations in a 1974 bilingual Spanish-Swedish anthology, *Mänskliga dikter* (Human poems), published by the now-defunct small press FiB:s Lyrikklubb.[13] A master of modernist lyric, Vallejo used poetry to compose absurd, grotesque, and even impossible images to represent the current state of humanity. An expanded collection of Vallejo's poetry appeared in *Uppfylld av världen* [Filled with the world], published by Stockholm's Forlaget Nordan in 1981 and introduced by the celebrated Swedish modernist writer and critic Artur Lundkvist.[14] This collection contained the translation of the poem that struck Andersson the most powerfully: "Traspié entre dos estrellas" ("Stumble between Two Stars," rendered in Swedish as "Snubblande mellan två stjärnor"), translated by Peter Landelius.[15] "It was his trivial images" that were so compelling, Andersson said later about why the poem made such a lasting impression. "But strangely enough, they don't feel trivial in the same way as triviality in life. It feels like an elevated, poeticized trivialism."[16] The poem's formal structure and the humanist ethos it embodies provide a poetic superstructure for *Songs from the Second Floor,* and the director dedicates the entire film to Vallejo at the outset. The poem's most repeated line, in Swedish "Älskade vare de som sätter sig" (Beloved are they who sit down), appears as white text against a black frame, along with "César Vallejo (1892–1938) In Memoriam," immediately prior to the film's opening credits. As Canadian scholar and independent filmmaker Dominique Russell has eloquently argued, *Songs* "echoes Vallejo's understanding of structure and time" (Russell 2008, 319). She cites the work of Spanish poetry scholar Américo Ferrari, who argues that Vallejo's *Human Poems* (*Poemas Humanos,* 1938), the posthumous collection in which the poem first appeared, "are constructed analogically, trying to understand 'a reality that resists rational understanding, and whose elusive meaning must be pinned down—though imperfectly—by the forced hammering of anaphora.'" Dating back to Greek lyrical tradition, "anaphora" is a poetic device whereby repeated words or phrases begin lines, resulting in a structure that "enhances the sense of the line even as it foregrounds the larger enumerative sequence" (Brogan 1993, 73). Nordic lyrical tradition has a similar device, called an *omkväde,* which dates back to the poetic *Edda,* a collection of Old Norse verse written in the thirteenth century (with some poems believed to date back as early as the ninth). In modern times, the *omkväde* has been used in everything from modern literature to the refrains of folk ballads, which Andersson has been known to use ironically, as a musical counterpoint, at darker moments in his films. "In literature there is that concept, to return with an *omkväde*," Andersson said in an interview. "I have tried to do this in a visual way, create an *omkväde*, or repetitions of the same subject, although perhaps in different forms."[17]

Such analogic repetition takes several forms in *Songs*. There is thematic repetition, or variations on an existential problem or social critique (as I discuss in the next chapter). There is visual repetition, such as the sequence of scenes in which different characters cannot sleep and sit, looking despondent, on the edge of their beds (as I'll discuss shortly). There is musical repetition through the use of *leitmotifs*, or distinctive musical phrases, that Benny Andersson's film score provides throughout (as I discuss later in this chapter). And there is verbal repetition, with the same or similar phrases of dialogue repeated in different scenes, often for tragicomedic effect. For example, in the scene immediately prior to Lasse the clerk getting fired in the corridor, we see him shining his shoes at home in his kitchen, where his wife tries to persuade him to stay home with her. He responds with a loosely quoted refrain from Ecclesiastes, chapter 3, "Everything has its time, darling,"—ironically, the very phrase the CEO had evoked in the film's opening scene when ordering Lasse's boss, Pelle, to fire more workers ("Everything has its time, Pelle"). When Lasse gets up to leave for work, his wife playfully blocks the doorway, saying, "No! No! No!" each time he tries to get around her. A few seconds later, in the firing scene, we see Lasse clinging to Pelle's legs in the corridor and crying "No! No! No!" in a desperate attempt to keep his boss from leaving. The repetition of this simple verbal phrase amplifies its impact, as there clearly is nothing playful or affectionate about this latter encounter.

The reappearance of certain characters also feels like a repetition, since rather than follow a main character's story, we instead encounter a motley ensemble of characters whom we "bump into again, and again, and again," as Andersson wrote in the project description. Most importantly, the film exercises analogic repetition through variations on similar images, such as an entire sequence of scenes that feature people sitting down. As Andersson explains, chuckling,

> The human being is tired and wants to rest awhile, and of course these people in this collage of sitting shots, they have been featured in earlier scenes of the film, and all of them have had something unfortunate happen to them. So it is like they sit down to get a little peace, a little relief, to rest and take a breather from their troubles.[18]

Among those who sit in the foreground of such scenes is Pelle, who sits on the edge of the bed later in the evening after having laid off workers. He fingers a broken golf club and looks distressed. His lover, Robert, standing in the background at the window wearing nothing but a T-shirt, comments on the traffic jam outside, then looks back at Pelle. As he turns, we see that his white T-shirt bears the red emblem "LO," the acronym for *Landsorganisationen i Sverige*, Sweden's largest umbrella labor organization.[19] Labor, in Andersson's film, is quite literally in bed with management, which perhaps accounts for the mass firings. "Pelle, what is with you?" Robert exclaims. Misreading the cause of Pelle's distress, he says, "We'll buy a new golf club. We'll buy a new one!" One of the subsequent seated scenes features Robert and Pelle sitting down in a restaurant. Next to him, against his seat, Pelle rests what appears to be a new golf club, wrapped in light blue packaging. We see only its distinct shape through the packaging's contours, which emphasizes how the golf club functions both as a symbol of Pelle's managerial class and as a fetishized object in a Marxist sense: while it presumably is meant to soothe Pelle's anguish, it of course has no inherent power to do so. Marx's concept of commodity fetishism, as presented in *Capital: A Critique of Political Economy* (1867), accounts for the transformation of the subjective and abstract aspects of economic value into objective, real things that are believed to hold intrinsic value. In the case of Pelle, his ability simply to replace his broken golf club with a new one not only implies that the people he is figuratively "breaking" and throwing out (by laying them off in the hundreds) are similarly expendable, but also that acquiring the new club was all he needed to soothe his existential anguish.

In fact, while Pelle seems calmer in the restaurant scene, now Robert is the one who appears anguished and withdrawn, implying that he has become aware of the mass firings. Then, another repetition: just as he did in the firing scene, Pelle looks straight into the camera—although here, he quickly looks back to the menu, trying to disregard the camera's gaze. He mumbles something to Robert and pats him on the hand as if to comfort him. This simple gesture is one that Russell claims is amplified through the film's stasis, constructed in part through the proliferation of sitting shots, since so little movement occurs within an individual scene. "Toning down movement heightens the significance of simple gestures," such as heaving a sigh or turning away in bed, she argues. Once again, the trivial becomes monumental, although focusing the viewer's attention on minutia for ninety-eight minutes can become exhausting. As Russell puts it, "The denial of the forward thrust of narrative in favor of analogic repetition contributes to the stasis of the film, most obviously set up by the static camera and the often static characters within its frame" (2008, 319). In the final moments of the restaurant scene, Pelle and the waiter look straight into the camera, for longer this time. Pelle seems annoyed and unsettled that he still is being watched; it is a new day, and he is ready to move on and enjoy a good meal. But the same unyielding gaze that saw him brutally fire Lasse the day before is now watching him eat in a restaurant with his lover and a new golf club by his side. "Those who look into the camera, they feel stripped naked, quite simply, and they are troubled by it," Andersson said in an interview. The repetition of Pelle's reversed gaze in multiple scenes, however, adds something more: the sense that he is dogged by guilt, which I discuss in the next chapter.

Songs was not Andersson's first attempt to render "Stumble between Two Stars" as a film. In 1982, he had begun a documentary tentatively titled *Beloved Are They Who Sit Down (Älskade vare de som sätter sig)* that sought to capture, in real life, many of the kinds of human moments Andersson later constructed in *Songs*. He even received funding for the project from Konstnärsnämnden (the Swedish Arts Grants Committee), a government agency that grants funding for art projects. Andersson ultimately decided that the project would work better as a fiction film and set it aside.[20] "When you write, you have many scenes that are extremely clear and then you try to find other scenes so that there will be a sense of unity," he later recalled in an interview with Swedish journalist Johanna Grönkvist. "It is quite simply a process that takes time." Two of the scenes featured in *Songs* had been clear in his mind for two decades, Andersson said: the scene where society sacrifices a young girl, and the one where a general celebrates his one hundredth birthday (Grönkvist 2000, 18). The two scenes in the film which quote from "Stumble between Two Stars" at length were not as easily formulated; in fact, Andersson's original idea was to have a character who was a poet wander in and out of the film's scenes and quote variations on the "Beloved is he who . . ." refrain. For example, a project description hand-dated November 1994 reads, "We can see a man standing with a floor lamp next to a taxi stand. Thereafter the poet appears in a rhetorical pause, beholds his attentive audience, and says, "Beloved is he who has bought a floor lamp."[21] As screen tests failed to produce a poet, Andersson and Borbás also became increasingly concerned that making a single character such a vital part of the film's structure would throw the film out of balance. The film was, after all, about what the poem communicates, and not about the character who reads it. Once they decided to have Stefan read the poem to his brother, they also deliberately left it unclear whether the poem is, in the world of the film, the poet's own words recited back to him, or a poem written by someone else. This, too, conspires to keep our focus on the poem's meaning rather than its performance.

The way in which the poem is evoked also facilitates this. The first of the two scenes that quote extensively from the poem opens in the corridor of the mental asylum. Kalle, a sixty-year-old furniture salesman, and his son, Stefan, are visiting Kalle's other son, Tomas (Peter Roth), the silent poet. As Tomas sits silently, his back to us, on a chair in the foreground, and Kalle stares despairingly out a window in the background, wailing that Tomas "wrote poems until he went nuts," Stefan crouches down facing his brother and soothingly recites to him certain lines from Vallejo's poem "Stumble between Two Stars":

>   beloved be the stranger and his wife,
>   and our neighbor with sleeves, collar, and eyes!
>   beloved be the one who sleeps on his back,
>   the one who wears a torn shoe in the rain
>   beloved be the bald man without hat
>   the one who catches a finger in the door
>   beloved is he who sweats of guilt or shame
>   he who pays with what he lacks
>   beloved are they who sit down[22]

Viewers may recognize these lines as a parody of the Beatitudes from the gospel according to Matthew. In the Biblical account, Jesus instructs his disciples in the core tenets of a radically new faith in the Sermon on the Mount, blessing the poor and declaring that the meek, not the powerful, shall inherit the earth.[23] Vallejo's poem replaces Christ's radical and divine act of blessing the lowliest in society with a radical and human act of loving others, even those whom society deems the least noteworthy, on the basis of their common humanity (Lindqvist 2010, 201).

The asylum scene, like all of the scenes in the film, is painstakingly composed, from the monochromatic color scheme to the interplay of "artificial" ceiling light and "natural" window light (all of it generated in-studio) to the receding layers of windows and doors down the long corridor, where orderlies struggle with a belligerent patient far in the background. Tomas sits quietly, arms folded, in the foreground, his back to the camera and turned slightly in a left profile. His silence seems to engulf the raised voices farther down the corridor. The total effect is that of a highly sanitary, brightly lit prison. As the scene unfolds, people walk in and out, but the focal point remains Tomas, even though he looks at no one, he says nothing, and his only movement is the slow heaving of his left side against his hand, showing that he is breathing. All Tomas does, for the duration of the scene, is sit, as his brother recites poetry to him. Together, they enact Vallejo's words "Beloved are they who sit down" (see figure 3.1).

In this scene, Andersson evokes another of his and Vallejo's common favored devices: that of the sight gag. Vallejo, like Andersson, believed in the power of the film medium as a way to showcase the human condition and authored a number of critical essays on film.[24] Vallejo, like Andersson, also had a great affinity for Charlie Chaplin, and he was writing a play about his contemporary at the time that he died in 1938 (Franco 1976, 278–79).[25] As the poet's biographer Jean

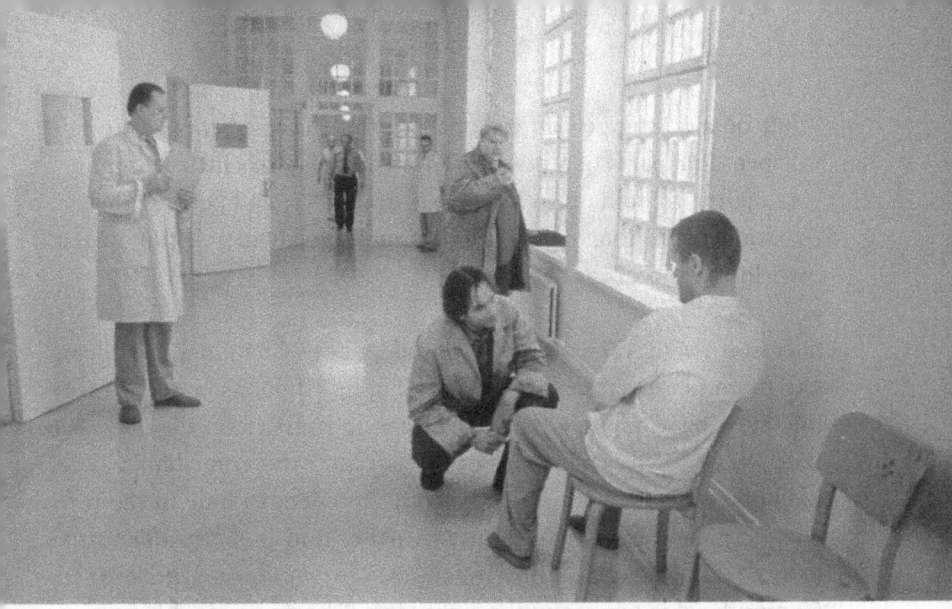

3.1 "The Dumb Brother—The Corridor." Shot in January 1999 at Studio 24. Stefan (Stefan Larsson) crouches in front of his mute older brother, Tomas (Peter Roth), an overly sensitive taxi driver who "wrote poems until he went nuts," and recites to him lines from Vallejo's poem "Stumble between Two Stars" as their portly father, Kalle (Lars Nordh), stares out a window in despair. Meanwhile, a doctor marches up the corridor to recover his lab coat, stethoscope, and file from a mental patient who has been silently posing as a doctor. The literary dialogue sews together these seemingly disparate elements. Photo courtesy of Studio 24; used with permission.

Franco observes, much like Chaplin, Vallejo dealt with the violent time in which they lived by highlighting the absurdity of ubiquitous human suffering in his art:

> The *Poemas humanos* are shot through with the sadness of the 1930s, when disasters were large and the human individual seemed of little account. Massed at fascist rallies, standing in

dole queues, shipped off to concentration camps, people were dispensable parts of a powerful system. Chaplin's little tramp, struggling to hold on to the shreds of dignity, had become the epitome of the lonely individual's tragi-comedy in a dehumanized world. (Franco 1976, 192)

Andersson's own tragicomedy, inspired by both Chaplin and Vallejo, seeks to emulate certain aspects of Chaplin's famous comical form while slowing Chaplin's famously frenetic pacing considerably. As Bazin wrote in his essay "Charlie Chaplin," the comedian would seize upon objects in his immediate environment to hide in the face of danger, such as burying himself in the sand in *The Adventurer* (1917) or camouflaging himself as a tree in *Shoulder Arms* (1918). "'Camouflage' is not really the right term," Bazin wrote. "It is more properly a form of mimicry," the art of imitating someone or something to entertain or ridicule (Bazin 1967c, 149). Chaplin's pursuers were often enemy soldiers or wardens, providing a sobering counterpoint that accentuated the absurdity and outrageousness of the films' physical comedy. And, of course, Chaplin used his own body as a comedic instrument, having it take on absurd new forms in his flight from authority figures. Rather than seek out talented actors who can perform physical comedy like Chaplin, Andersson instead casts actors whose bodies, voices, and presence naturally construct the physical comedic elements the scene requires. Andersson's emulation of these Chaplinesque comic forms is perhaps best exemplified in the asylum corridor scene when Stefan recites poetry to his brother.

As Stefan recites "Beloved be the bald man without hat / the one who catches a finger in the door," Kalle, the boisterous and portly father, turns impatiently and interrupts Stefan: "Caught a fing— what's so remarkable about that? Everyone's done it you know! He wrote poetry until he went nuts!" to which Stefan responds, "Calm down!" Here, Kalle denigrates both the poem's philosophical overtones and the poet's art, unwittingly demonstrating that it was not his son's devotion to poetry that silenced him but rather a brutal and materialistic society that fails to value either arts or humanity. It is also Kalle, not Tomas, who appears to be the most visibly and audibly disturbed, raising the question of which of them is crazy and who is truly sane. As Stefan turns back toward Tomas, a man wearing professional dress clothes and flanked by two orderlies hurries up the corridor behind them and stops in front of a doctor in a white coat who, we suddenly realize, had been standing there quietly the entire time, just to Stefan's left, but had until this moment been "camouflaged" by the other elements in the corridor scene. Now that the man accosting him has drawn our attention to this silent figure, we notice that he wears a stethoscope and leafs through the pages of a manila folder. Just as Stefan recites to Tomas "Beloved is he who sweats with guilt—" the hurried man asks the doctor sternly, "What kind of stupidity is this?" We then realize, as the hurried man and the orderlies remove the silent doctor's folder, his stethoscope, and his white coat, that he was never a doctor at all, but a mental patient dressed up in the real doctor's trappings. Stefan's poetic line about guilt in the foreground is timed perfectly to coincide with the exposure of the false doctor's identity in the background. Stefan turns to look at the "real" and "false" doctors briefly, then turns back to Tomas and continues reciting, "he who pays with what he lacks"—just as the "real" doctor searches for his wallet in his recovered lab coat. He says accusingly to the patient, "There was a wallet here too—where is it?" then finds it in his own pants pocket and hurries away. The idea that we cannot trust our authority figures to be who they seem to be, much less to exercise competence or responsibility in their craft, recurs in the film (most absurdly when a magician severely wounds an audience volunteer while attempting to saw him in half).

Finally, as Stefan concludes his recitation, "Beloved are they who sit down," Kalle loses his temper completely and yells, "Sit down! What's with that? Beloved are they who sit down?! Why should one love them?! Look at your brother! *He sits where he sits!*" Two orderlies drag Kalle screaming from the corridor, again suggesting that it is Kalle, not Tomas, who is the crazy one. Kalle's parting yell from the doorway is "He sits where he sits! Who's going to love him then?" The line "he sits where he sits!"—a line penned by Andersson, not Vallejo—serves two functions. First, it has Kalle, the film's spokesperson for Western capitalist middle-class values, flying into a rage over the implication that the trivial act of sitting—the opposite of working, being industrious, or contributing to society—could be so significant that one writes an entire poem about it. "Our established culture, they get embarrassed reading about trivial things," Andersson said in an interview.[26] Second, Kalle's question "Who's going to love him then?" suggests that Tomas's failure to contribute to society and support his family through work that earns money renders him useless and unlovable. The contrast between Kalle, the self-absorbed father who is unable to show concern or love for his son, and Stefan, the poetry-reciting brother who can and does, could not be clearer. Kalle gets thrown out on the family's next visit to Tomas as well, this time screaming, "Is there no one who can help you?!" even though Kalle seems at least as in need of mental health intervention as Tomas. As Nordh said later about his character, "They locked up the wrong one."[27] In the third and final visit to the mental asylum—the next-to-last scene in the film—Stefan visits Tomas without Kalle, who as we soon find out is preoccupied by the failure of his latest business venture and haunted by an old dead friend to whom he'd owed money.

Andersson said that he'd initially added some lines of his own to Vallejo's "beloved" repetitions but then took them out, deciding that Vallejo's words were all that were needed. In choosing which of the poem's unrhymed forty-five lines to use in the dialogue, Andersson chose those he believed to be "extremely clear and simple." He explained,

> [Vallejo] sometimes has very difficult formulations. In that poem, there are several lines that are nearly cryptic, and I like the ones that are more straightforward and open, that are extremely easy to understand, because they are enough. I'm thinking of the line "Beloved be the one who carries a shoe in the rain." Sure, it is beautiful, but it isn't very clear or obvious. One thinks, the one who carries a shoe in the rain, has he lost his shoe, or—?[28]

The lines from Vallejo's poem that Stefan recites during his final asylum visit are timed to coincide with other trivial events going on in the space of the room simultaneously. And, like most scenes in the film, they also reiterate bits of dialogue and themes presented in other scenes. He begins:

> Beloved be the one who works by the day, by the month, by the hour
> Beloved be the one who sweats in guilt or shame
> The person who at the order of his hands goes to the movies
> The one who pays with what he lacks
> The one who sleeps on his back

At this point, Tomas, who is lying on his back in the asylum bed in the foreground, begins to cry, which can be interpreted as the despair of the artist who finds beauty in the poetry that he cannot find in life. The figure of a man lying on his back in a hospital bed, with a family member sitting beside him, features also in a much earlier scene, in which an immigrant who was beaten up by hooligans on the street lies wounded on a hospital bed in the hallway, which he shares with other patients since the hospital is overcrowded. Because we never get to know these men who have ended up in hospitals, what connects them is their condition. As Russell points out, "Poses are repeated, creating a mosaic of 'everyman' in which characters are interchangeable" (2008, 318). Stefan continues his recitation from the poem, saying, "He who no longer remembers his childhood." At this point, his girlfriend tells him to stop, saying, "You'll make him sad. You mustn't be sad, Tomas. You mustn't cry," which seems a ridiculous thing to say in such a situation, perhaps all the more so because we've heard it said plenty of times in similar situations. Stefan comforts Tomas by saying, "Take it easy, Tomas. It doesn't matter. Beloved is he who sits down."

At this point, two mental patients against the window in the background, one sitting and one standing, begin comparing Tomas to Jesus and asserting Jesus's humanity, building on a similarly nonsensical conversation they'd begun in the previous asylum scene. They conclude that Tomas, like Jesus, was sad because he had no business concepts, that Jesus was tortured and crucified because he was a nice person, and that Tomas also was a nice person. While they don't say it, the next step in this theorem would be to assert that Tomas, too, is being tortured and crucified by society for being a nice person, a notion reinforced with Stefan's next poetic line of dialogue: "Beloved be the righteous one without thorns." In this scene, then, as well as throughout the film, the timing of analogic repetitions is crucial both to Andersson's tragicomedy and to the scathing humanist critiques it contains.

In Vallejo's poems, seemingly trivial moments possess enormous symbolic and religious content, even while they question the benevolence of God and the redemption of humankind. The poem featured in *Songs* laments a loss of *Logos* (the divine word, or reason incarnate in Jesus Christ) through the poetic trivialization of Jesus's Sermon on the Mount (Franco 1976, 35).[29] For example, a line from the Beatitudes parody that Stefan quotes in the film, "The one who wears a watch and has seen God," articulates the mortality, even the impending death, of a man whose time has run out and who soon will meet his maker. But this language also paradoxically negates the divinity of God, who can be apprehended by a person wearing a watch. The trivializing language of this poetic description paradoxically strips away the divine mystery of the God incarnate (the Word made flesh in Jesus Christ, who was both human and divine) while associating Godlike power with worldly time. The man's life is subject primarily not to God's authority but to that of worldly forces standing in for God. Vallejo's poem likewise renders the Beatitudes ineffective as divine speech by trivializing the nobility and exceptionality of the saved. In this poem, people are beloved simply because they *are*; their identities ("the one who has no birthdays") and their actions ("Beloved [be] the people who sit down") are otherwise too commonplace to matter. These tautological declarations interrogate not only the parental love of a divine God who tends to his believers' needs but also humanity's love for the lowliest among us.

Film and Painting

While Callot's etching *The Hanging* (figure 1.3) is the image Andersson claims to fear most, it has plenty of challengers among the ample art books that fill the shelves on Studio 24's second floor. As the poet W. H. Auden writes of the world's great master painters in "Musée des Beaux Arts" (1940): "About suffering they were never wrong."[30] The only art work Auden's poem references explicitly is Bruegel's *Landscape with the Fall of Icarus* (*De val van Icarus*, 1558), in which the eye must look hard for the fallen Icarus since none of the other figures in the expansive landscape seems to have noticed that a boy has just fallen out of the sky to his death. (In the lower right-hand corner of the canvas, a man can be observed reaching toward a pair of bare legs protruding from the water.) Bruegel's landscapes have provided much inspiration for Andersson's complex images; as Andersson said in an interview, they "are stories about the human condition, even if there are, most often, no main characters in the paintings. In that way Bruegel is unique, but there are of course other Masters [in whose work] you do see main characters, although they are wide images."[31] Many such images from Andersson's art books have manifested themselves in all three films of his humanist trilogy. Each of the films has, however, an aesthetic unity, not least through a monochromatic color scheme—Andersson says he favors green because it has so many shades—and his use of geometry to create similar perceptions of angle and depth (ibid). As Russell notes, the first eight shots of *Songs* feature almost exclusively straight lines; it is not until the hapless magician's scene that Andersson introduces curves through a circular stage and small round tables in the audience (2008, 321). Thus while the paintings of many great artists are referenced in *Songs,* Andersson remains the "master" of this filmic work—as evidenced by his meticulous "touching up" of scenes to satisfy his vision. "We have re-taken half of the images that appear in the film, and I don't see anything strange about that," he said after the film's release. "In the art of painting, you repaint and make as many changes as you like. Why can't you do the same thing with the art of film?" (Viklund 2000, 12).

While Andersson had childhood ambitions to become a painter, he has contented himself with the time-intensive work of painting expansive and meticulous film sets alongside his crew. He said that he remains envious of the art of painting, however, because viewers are prepared to linger with a work of art in a way they resist having to do with a film. "People go into museums and look at how some artists have sought to capture, or describe, their view of life and existence. It is fantastic that a person can stand for a long time and look at a single painting, isn't it?"[32] Andersson doesn't fault viewers for not expecting to spend as much time pondering filmic images, since most films don't demand this. But in an interview with a Swedish journalist published around the time of *Songs*' Swedish premiere, Andersson sought to prime audiences to expect something different from his film:

> The art of film has seldom shown us examples of powerful and challenging images. There are only a handful of films that I would like to see again. When it comes to painting, however, there are a ton of paintings I would gladly see again. I have, with my film, sought to reconquer the power of the moving image by refining simplicity. (Viklund 2000, 12)

None of the art works referenced in *Songs* functions in isolation, and, in fact, more than one painting inspired certain scenes, such as the sacrifice scene. All of them, however, meet Andersson's criteria for complex images that foster extended contemplation on the human condition.

Arguably the film's most recognizable art historical reference is Simberg's *Wounded Angel* (*Haavoittunut enkeli*, 1903; figure 3.2). In 2006, the Finnish public voted it Finland's national painting in a contest conducted by the Finnish National Gallery Ateneum, where the painting is housed.[33] As Anne Karhio has pointed out, while those familiar with the artist know that he was recovering from a nerve disease when he painted it, the artist himself has never sought to contextualize the painting's image (2012, 27). Karhio writes, "The absence of particular context, and the fascination with the painting's depiction of unspecified sorrow, have also made it possible for artists and writers from other cultures to engage with Simberg's work" (29). This "unspecified sorrow" made the painting an ideal source of inspiration for Andersson's film.

Simberg's painting depicts two boys carrying a blindfolded angel on a wooden stretcher against a mostly barren landscape with a lake in the background. The boy in front looks straight ahead, but the boy in the rear looks to his left, straight at the viewer, with an anguished expression. The angel does not look ethereal, but earthly; aside from her long white feathered wings, which bear faint marks of a wound, she looks like a girl, barefoot, blonde, her head bowed and her body hunched over in a seated position, clutching the edges of the stretcher. Clenched between her right hand and the stretcher are a small bouquet of the same delicate white wildflowers that grow close to the path. The painting features muted colors that also denote earthbound mourning, with browns, pale blues, and black contrasting with the white of the angel and the flowers. All of the painting's visual cues cast the angel as a human innocent who has been critically wounded, rather than a cosmic one. As Karhio writes, "His painting serves as a perfect citation for highlighting the universal human condition of sorrow and suffering" (2012, 30).

Songs evokes Simberg's painting in the figure of a young girl whom all of society's leaders have chosen to sacrifice, presumably to appease the economic gods. The scene, titled "The Sacrifice" (figure 3.3), opens to a landscape as expansive as a Bruegel painting, albeit with all of its objects locked in stasis. Thousands of people are gathered atop a high plateau circling a steep cliff with a wide wooden plank suspending over its edge. The plank's wood is the same pale color as that of the angel's stretcher in Simberg's painting. In the left foreground stand a line of religious leaders in gilded ceremonial robes, their miters and croziers denoting the rank of bishop or archbishop,

3.2 Hugo Simberg (Finland, 1873–1917), *The Wounded Angel* (*Haavoittunut enkeli*, 1903). Oil on canvas, 127 x 154 cm. This blindfolded angel inspired the sacrificed girl in Andersson's film; the boy's anguished look connects with the viewer's gaze just as Andersson's film characters often do. Held at the Finnish National Museum Ateneum, which provided the photograph; used with permission.

all of them facing forward, waiting. In the right foreground, also facing forward looking and waiting, stand society's learned men in black suits and top hats, and behind them, military leaders in dress uniforms. Closest to the plank, in the middle of the shot, stand what is supposed to be Sweden's royal family wearing dark suits. The figure that is meant to be Queen Silvia is recognizable primarily through her hair color and style, body type and self-possessed stance, and dress style; we never get close enough to see her face. In the deep background, there is a clump of bright red banners—long associated with the workers' movement—among the spectators. Next to the plank, at the cliff's edge, a safety rope is strung between two stakes in the ground, presumably to protect the illustrious leaders standing nearby. The doctor, and then the psychologist, enter the frame in the right foreground, slowly walking backwards, leading the procession. Soon, Andersson's version of the "wounded angel" appears: a young blonde girl, barefoot, blindfolded, and dressed in a plain white gown, is led into the frame by her parents, who also wear dark gray suits. Halfway to the plank they stop and hug their daughter, who is then led to the plank's edge by another gray-suited man. He steps back and the "queen" steps cautiously onto the plank, a rope tied around her waist and held by an attendant as a safety measure. As she firmly pushes the girl over the edge, the girl gives a shriek that is silenced by the cavern that swallows her (where she presumably has fallen to her death). The queen steps gingerly back to her entourage as the crowd stands in stunned silence.

This scene, on its own arguably as enigmatic as Simberg's painting, is clarified somewhat by the scenes preceding it and the one directly after it. In the first scene in this sequence, two workers in construction gear are stacking enormous jagged rocks at the base of the steep cliff, the significance of which will become clear in the ensuing scenes. The only line of dialogue—in another repetitive, trivialist

3.3 "The Sacrifice." Elaborate exterior shot on the Swedish island of Gotland, October 1998. Society's leaders and followers gather to sacrifice a young girl, Anna (Helene Mathiasson), to appease the economic gods. Andersson deemed this limestone quarry the only suitable site in Sweden for this scene. Photo courtesy of Studio 24; used with permission.

move—comes when one of the workers gets his finger caught in the rocks and yells, "Ah! I'm stuck!" and his coworker helps him get loose (a variation on the train station scene in which a man gets his finger caught in the door). As the workers walk away, one nursing his hurt finger, a man in a dark suit looks up and signals with his hand. A test dummy comes hurtling down onto the rocks, and its midsection splits open. The man in the dark suit looks over at a crew of medical workers standing ready next to a minivan with its rear hatch open. They retrieve the dummy with a stretcher—another allusion to Simberg's painting—and after two doctors "inspect" the dummy's fake wound and appear satisfied, they load it into the minivan. To the right of the frame, a crowd of people wearing suits stands poker-straight in the mud, facing the jagged rocks, watching; their cars are parked in the deep background, at the base of the high plateau encircling the scene. (I discuss the role of these "silent witnesses" more in the next chapter.) This scene helps construct one of the "hidden dimensions" Julian Hanich has argued pervades the film's complex images.[34] In the sacrifice scene, we never see the falling girl crushed on the jagged rocks below. But because we'd seen, in this scene, an objective demonstration of exactly what would happen to her, our imaginations are provoked to conjure a more horrifying image in our minds than anything Andersson could show us. This horror is amplified by the realization that those who carefully rehearsed the sacrifice in advance had presumably made this connection in their minds and yet done nothing to stop it from happening. Or worse, they never made the connection at all but just unthinkingly carried out their assigned tasks. The scene concludes with the man who orchestrated the rehearsal looking at his watch—both a sign of cruel objectivity and a reference to Vallejo's poem.

For those familiar with Simberg's painting, the mental image of a dead "angel" lying on a stretcher, rather than a wounded, sitting one, transforms the sorrow of Simberg's image to something closer to horror and outrage at the death of an innocent. The director said in an interview that the reason for creating such images is both to express and to awaken outrage: "History is full of cruelty and brutality and it isn't possible, of course, to avoid depicting these dark sides of existence, those horrible sides of existence, there are many artists who do that. You do it out of a kind of fascination mixed with fear, because actually you don't want it to happen, injustice, killing, etc."[35] The visual and thematic inspiration for the sacrifice itself—the act of pushing someone off a cliff—comes from a different early twentieth-century painting: Nils Dardel's *Execution* (*Exekution*, 1919; figure

3.4). The clearest visual citation is the distinctive physical features of the landscape where the "execution" is taking place: a high plateau with sheer sides. Andersson's team searched all over Sweden for a suitable site and finally found a limestone quarry near the town of Slite (population 1,500) on the island of Gotland that Andersson deemed suitable.[36] In the painting, a boorish executioner in a bright red vest kicks a thin young man backward over the cliff. The young man, wearing a white suit and holding up a cross, is represented here as a vulnerable innocent—and physically resembles Dardel himself. The artist depicts the executioner in the painting as Gustaf Oscar Wallenberg, a Swedish government official who forced his daughter to break her engagement to Dardel (Asplund 1957). Like the other complex images Andersson is drawn to, *Execution* is marked by depth of field, multiple figures, and multiple actions. In the background, around the curve of the cliff, there is another execution in progress that mirrors the one in the foreground; only the colors of the figures' clothes are different (the condemned man in the background is wearing black). The other figures in the painting, associated with the executioners through their brightly colored clothing, appear unfazed by what is happening around them. One of them, leading a horse, looks dispassionately at the execution in the foreground, and the other, standing just to the right of the execution scene, turns his head away, so that he is looking outside the frame.

This scene is one of two scenes in *Songs* that Andersson claimed he had clearly formulated in his mind for twenty years. But by the time he got around to filming *Songs,* Andersson's dark satire in this scene had narrowed its focus from existential human failures writ large to the economic crisis of the 1990s, when unemployment rates tripled in Sweden and many young people struggled for years to establish themselves on the job market. This is why archetypes of leaders from all sectors of society are implicated in the sacrifice

scene; Andersson believes they "sacrificed an entire generation" with short-sighted, market-driven economic policies and social leadership (a critique I return to in the next chapter).[37] Interestingly, Borbás initially objected to Queen Silvia, a popular and sympathetic figure among Swedes, being the one to push the child over the cliff, but Andersson wasn't swayed (Göransson 2000, 84). "The queen stood as a symbol for the power-holding class in society which is responsible for society's development," Andersson said later. "There were many who suffered for years" following the economic crisis of 1992–93, he said, "and then there are those who were not affected by the tough economy but rather lived well in spite of it. Those belonged to, among others, the royal family, who often are used when you need to inaugurate something, have a large ceremony."[38]

The painter whose work resonates the most with Andersson, however, is Otto Dix, fierce satirist of what he saw as a morally bankrupt urban society in Germany during the Weimar Republic.[39] He and another of Andersson's favorite painters, George Grosz (1893–1959), were associated with the avant-garde movement known as *Neue Sachlichkeit*, or New Objectivity, whose work art historians describe as marked by "a radical rejection of all emotional bias, a deliberately cultivated unsentimentality" (Schmalenbach 1940, 164). Dix had volunteered at the front during the First World War, and art historian G. H. Hamilton describes his subsequent paintings as "perhaps the most powerful as well as the most unpleasant anti-war

3.4 (opposite page) Nils Dardel (Sweden, 1888–1943), *Execution* (Exekution, 1919). Oil on canvas, 130 cm x 115 cm. This postimpressionist painting provided the inspiration for the film's sacrifice scene, both in terms of the cliff's sheer features and the religious symbolism. This painting is privately owned, and the image is in the public domain.

statements in modern art" (Dempsey 2002, 249). As Maria Tatar (1995) has observed, Dix's and Grosz's paintings express both the horrors of war and the horrors of the decadent Weimar Republic society that followed it. Dix returned home from the war determined that his art would showcase, in the most vulgar, unsanitized form, everything that was wrong with society, "to convince people and improve social conditions in the only way that was still possible, by confronting them with 'facts, stark, brutal facts'" (Eberle 1985, 50). This stark, stylized, and cruel hyper-reality is precisely Andersson's aim with the aesthetics of the desolate urban landscapes and monochromatic interiors in *Songs from the Second Floor*. As Christopher Mildren puts it, "The urban scenes are shot in a textural and tonal palette that is cold, hard and carefully controlled" (2013, 152). Dix also pursued this aesthetic in his portraiture. As art historian Edward M. Gómez writes, "Dix tended to depict his human subjects—female nudes, businessmen and figures from the Weimar era's nocturnal demimonde—with a candor that presented them as deeply vulnerable, pathetic, grotesque, ugly or worse. In Dix's work of the 1920s, reality did not only bite—often it could startle or even repel a viewer, too" (2010, 65). Small wonder, then, that the scene in *Songs* that is arguably the most vulgar and repulsive is modeled after Dix's work—and set in Stockholm's stately Grand Hôtel (or rather, a stylized version of it).

In a festival publication distributed at a retrospective of Roy Andersson's films shown at the Bergamo Film Meeting in Italy in 2003, an image of Dix's oil painting *To Beauty* (*An die Schönheit*, 1922, figure 3.5) is featured alongside a still from the film's Grand Hotel scene (Girola and Fornara 2003, 70–71). (The publication also features a reproduction of Dix's grotesque etching *Three Nudes on the Beach* (*Drei mädchenakte am strand*, 1923)—and indeed, the handful of naked or half-naked bodies we see in *Songs* are decidedly unglamorous, from Lasse's naked wife to Robert's wide derriere.) Dix's title *To Beauty* is ironic, as the brothel featured in the painting is anything but beautiful. The artist places himself front and center in the painting holding a telephone, which Sergiusz Michalski has argued "indicates that he sees himself as a reporter, communicating facts, completely devoted to the objects and events of reality" (1998, 54). Dressed sharply in a gray suit and sporting a closely cropped haircut, Dix is gazing at the viewer with a stern expression on his face, his rigid bodily stance registering his condemnation of the decadent surroundings, which recede far into the darkened background. In the left foreground is a heavily made-up woman, presumably a prostitute, leaning forward to emphasize her ample bust line. Behind her dances a flapper and a man who looks either intoxicated or asleep. Behind Dix, a maniacally grinning black jazz drummer with an American flag protruding from his breast pocket pumps a fist into the air, and an image of an American Indian in a feathered headdress is painted on the drum's canvas. Their presence in the painting would seem to underscore the fetishization of so-called exotic and primitive cultures—in particular, jazz music—that was prevalent among bohemians during the Weimar period. Behind the drummer, a woman sways to the music wearing nothing but her corset, cinched tight to plump up her bosom. The scene is a cabaret of the grotesque.

With *Songs*' "Misgivings I, Grand Hotel" scene (figure 3.6), Andersson emulates his favorite painter's propensity to capture the vulgarity and moral bankruptcy of modern society.[40] The fact that the scene, in the script, is given a roman numeral both marks it as one of several variations on a given theme—part of Andersson's repetitive strategy—and reinforces the film's intermedial character. ("Misgivings II, Airport" is the scene late in the film in which moneyed elites drag their heavy baggage through an departure hall, abandoning the misery they've wrought.) The Grand Hotel scene completes

the sequence of scenes surrounding the sacrifice, and it is as visually revolting as the sacrifice scene is existentially horrifying. Once again, Andersson accentuates the scene's grotesqueness by evoking contrasts with an earlier scene, in this case, the one immediately preceding the sacrifice. In the earlier scene, the psychologist questions the girl, Anna, in the presence of society's most learned men and women in a spacious and elegant salon with tapestries on the walls and a high ceiling, evoking a grand room of Europe's historic universities and castles. The room's interior architecture features ornamental, gilded decor and furniture typical of Sweden's Oscarian period of the nineteenth century. Anna's parents stand in the background, and behind them hangs a wall-length tapestry with a portrait of a nobleman (his face is out of the camera frame, rendering him an archetype). There is a Persian rug on the floor. Anna (Helene Matthiasson) stands, hands clasped in front of her, at the center of the room, and the psychologist (Stenfeldt), in a gray suit, sits in a gilded chair next to her holding a notebook. She speaks slowly and deliberately in an infantilizing tone, asking the girl if she has read any books and informing her that "these old women and old men here (she looks around the room at elderly scholars dressed in dark suits, then turns back to Anna),

3.5   (opposite page) Otto Dix (Germany, 1891–1969), *To Beauty* (An die Schönheit, 1922). Oil on canvas, 140 cm x 122 cm. Dix was an expressionist painter of the Neue Sachlichkeit, or New Objectivity movement. Andersson has declared Dix his favorite painter and the Neue Sachlichkeit a major influence on his own work. Studio 24 paired this image with one of the film's Grand Hotel set (see figure 3.6) in its film festival brochures. The painting is held at the Von der Heydt-Museum in Wuppertal, Germany, and its copyright is held by the Artists Rights Society (ARS), New York, and VG Bild-Kunst, Bonn, who provided the photograph; used with permission.

they have read ALL the books." She continues, "And when one has read that much, one also knows a lot. Then one knows how to do things and what one can do—and Anna, there is one more thing one knows when one has read so much. One knows what cannot be done, what is impossible. An ant, for example, cannot eat up an elephant. It's impossible." The psychologist's soliloquy is punctuated by short, Beckettian-style commentaries from various old men sitting around the room, who affirm the veracity of her words. It's clear that Anna has been chosen for a task that society's learned ones deem to be of grave importance, and it's equally clear they have an absurdly overinflated notion of their own knowledge, wisdom, and experience. The grim consequences of their ignorance become apparent in the next scene, when society sacrifices the child Anna to an unnamed god in the hope that this will restore prosperity—a ritual usually associated with pre-Christian, pagan religions. This is what happens, the film suggests, when we reject the redeeming aspects of the European Enlightenment's intellectual heritage—which is what gave rise to our universities and the study of the humanities—and embrace instead the false, modern gods that capitalist society has conjured.

The Grand Hotel scene, which immediately follows the sacrifice, features the same people and similarly stately decor, but the environment and the mood are decadent and vulgar, as all of society apparently seeks to drown its guilt in booze. The pillars of society are now slouched in leather chairs or perched on high stools in the hotel's ornate bar. On an architectural column to the left is an ornate, gilded cross that has the queen's head, wearing a crown, mounted on it in the place of a crucifix, casting her as a symbol of worship and devotion. Beneath it sit a decorated military officer on one side, and on the other, a bishop, resting his crozier against the column. The doctor in his white coat stands at the end of the bar next to a seated woman in traditional folk dress, and a man drags the red banner of the worker's movement behind him

3.6 "Misgivings I, Grand Hotel." Shot in November 1998 at Studio 24. The child psychologist (Eva Stenfeldt) is too drunk to pull herself up onto her barstool, and the elderly scholar beside her vomits, then repeats the rhetorical phrase, "We have sacrificed the flower of youth. What more can we do?" Photo courtesy of Studio 24; used with permission.

on the floor. In the foreground to the right, the psychologist (Stenfeldt) struggles haplessly, as if very drunk, to pull herself up onto a bar stool, and a learned old man, his tuxedo draped in a medal denoting academic honors, vomits onto the bar. The psychologist and the old man numbly repeat variations on the same lines of dialogue, over and over:

Psychologist: I can't get up!
Old Man: We have sacrificed the bloom of youth. What more can we do?

Their dull repetitions imply that they are traumatized by their participation in Anna's death. Society's leaders are trapped in this gruesome scene—physically stuck, since their bodies are collapsing, and metaphysically stuck as well, since they realize they cannot hope for the redemption they'd sought by sacrificing the girl. The scholar's repeated line "What more can we do?" is rhetorical and ironic, as they have committed the worst moral crime possible: the murder of an innocent. The film's archetypal reproduction of the actual Grand Hôtel in Stockholm encapsulates the building's symbolic value for Sweden's national traditions; for example, the illustrious Nobel Banquet—an annual event celebrating the world's greatest scholars and writers—was held in the hotel's Spegelsalen (Mirror Room) from 1901 to 1929, when the event became too large and was moved to Stockholm City Hall.[41] Still today, Nobel laureates are housed at the hotel, and they are serenaded on Sweden's most revered national holiday, Saint Lucia Day, December 13, by girls wearing white and bearing candles in the honor of a Sicilian saint (a young girl who was killed—one could say, "sacrificed"—by society's elders for refusing to renounce her religious beliefs). Over the course of its history, the hotel's other esteemed guests have included civil rights leader Martin Luther King, Princess Grace and Prince Rainier of Monaco, American singer Frank Sinatra, and film icon Greta Garbo, among others. The Grand Hotel's visual elegance, its elevated place in Sweden's most cherished traditions, and its historic function in hosting world leaders and scholars makes Andersson's filmic degradation of this culturally "sacred" space all the more powerful and grotesque.

Film and Music

In the corridor scene discussed earlier in this chapter, Kalle's opening words to his son Tomas, the poet, in the mental asylum are, "Is it the same old tune today, too?"[42] Kalle uses a musical metaphor to pose a rhetorical question, criticizing his son's inability to communicate. But the point is that there is no music coming from Tomas; he has been struck dumb and locked up. This irony manifests itself in the title of the film, *Songs from the Second Floor,* a name chosen early in the production when the poet was conceived as a central character—with extensive speaking lines—who lived in a second-floor apartment. Once Andersson and his team had silenced the poet, so to speak, they wondered what the title now could refer to—and realized that both Andersson's Studio 24 office and his own apartment were located on the second floor.[43] In a kind of self-referential, Felliniesque move, the "songs" of the film's title thus became Andersson's own artistic ruminations on the state of mankind.

Music plays an important role in all of Andersson's films, and not merely as a metaphor. Sometimes it serves as a grotesque counterpoint to underscore scathing social commentary in his austere, unyielding images. One of Andersson's self-named obsessions—well known among Swedish journalists and film practitioners—is the idyllic, nationalist Swedish folk music of the 1930s and '40s, music that was popular during his own childhood, while the Nazis were perpetuating genocide in a neighboring country whose language and culture were quite similar to Sweden's. In his award-winning, unfinished short film *Something Has Happened* (*Någonting har hänt,* 1987) about the HIV virus, for example, a soundtrack of Swedish folk singer Edvard Persson singing "Scanian Castles and Manors" (*Skånska slott och herresäten*), written by the poet Hjalmar Gullberg, can be heard during a scene in which Nazi scientists are forcing an emaciated prisoner into an ice bath with a pile of bodies lying nearby. The melody, and Persson's voice, are folksy and upbeat, matching the optimism of the lyrics, which romanticize not only the Scanian landscape but also the social relations of its inhabitants by suggesting that the sun shines equally on the rich and the poor. "The reason Edvard Persson gets to sing that song during a scene that shows deadly experiments with cold done on Jews, is that this song was unbelievably popular during the time the mental preparation for that eradication was going on," Andersson wrote in *Our Time's Fear of Seriousness*. "It was the golden age of burlesque comedy. There was no trace of what was going on in our song or film repertoire" (2009, 77). Indeed, the 1930s in Sweden is often called the decade of "Pilsner films"—light-hearted comedies designed to help people escape the social, political, and economic turbulence of the Depression era.

Andersson had intended to use Persson's folk music in *Songs* as well. But Swedish composer Benny Andersson (no relation to Roy), whom the director initially invited to compose the music for the film's culminating scene, decided that he wanted to score the entire film. "When Benny Andersson sensed that he would be competing with [Persson's] music, he said, I'm going to do the rest, too—so he did," the filmmaker said.[44] Benny Andersson, who achieved world fame as part of the 1970s pop group ABBA and subsequently pursued a career as a respected composer and the conductor of Benny Anderssons Orkester, said in an interview that he did not know Roy personally before the director contacted him on the recommendation of Kalle Boman, a mutual colleague. But he knew "his good reputation as a brave and headstrong artist."[45] The composer, who declares that Roy Andersson is a "musical person," came to Studio 24 to watch clips from the film and get a sense of what the film team was looking for. Benny Andersson had composed film music before (for example, the opening score for a filmed version of Astrid Lindgren's children's classic *Mio My Son (Mio min Mio)*, but he had never seen a film like Roy Andersson's before. "It's a fantastic film," he said later. "Like a reminder of how infernal everything is in our time. Sad, funny, and beautiful. I don't know how he does it." When the composer first saw the unfinished film, however, his initial reaction was that it didn't need music to accentuate the images. "But Roy didn't relent so easily, so I presented a theme for him"—one that the composer had already written—"and he jumped at it." The finished score—the slow, jolting pulse of bass strings in a waltz tempo contrasted with a lighter, cautiously playful, melody—exemplifies both the style and the thematics of *Songs*. "Roy often said that he wanted it to 'stumble forward' [*stappla fram*] in places, and I tried to accommodate him the best I could," composing everything on his Synclavier, Benny Andersson said. These "stumbles" in the music, of course, correspond to the title and theme of Vallejo's poem "Stumble between Two Stars" (the word for "stumble" in the Swedish title of the poem, *snubbla*, is a synonym for *stappla*). The musical score's slow and heavily lurching baseline also mimics the universal heaviness and awkwardness of the characters' gestures, as well as the inexplicably heavy stop-and-go traffic throughout the film, contributing to the film's intentional stasis. But the lightness and playfulness of the slightly quicker melody reassures us that there is humor and hope to be found in these dark times. "I didn't think at the time that [the film] was particularly comical, but I actually do now, even if the laughter always gets stuck in my throat," Benny Andersson wrote in an email. "Inscrutable, that Roy."[46]

Benny Andersson also composed the music for a hymn featured in the sacrifice scene, "The Time of Love," (Kärlekens tid), written by well-known Swedish psalmist Ylva Eggehorn and performed by Helen Sjöholm. In the scene, once the queen has pushed Anna off the cliff and returned to her place, over muted sobs a recording of

Eggehorn's hymn comes wafting over the crowd. This hymn, too, "stumbles," in its execution, since some in the crowd sing along but do not keep tempo with the professional recording ostensibly playing from the loudspeakers erected on a pole. In the English subtitled versions of the film, the words to the song are not translated for viewers. The words to the hymn, while faint, are distinguishable to Swedish-speaking viewers—particularly to those who subsequently purchased the Benny Anderssons Orkester CD featuring the song (released by Mono Music in 2004). In the hymn itself, the supplicant prays to God for comfort, love, and connection, and a sense of purpose. But in the film, those joining in the hymn playing over the loudspeaker are trying in vain to transcend the horror of the senseless act they just perpetuated, or at least try to find some purpose, truth, or reconciliation—a "song"—for it all. The faith and hope expressed in the hymn's music and lyrics provide a counterpoint for the desperation and fear that led an entire society to murder an innocent child (and sacrifice the entire generation she represents), and for the crippling guilt that follows that act (which I discuss in the next chapter). The god that demands the sacrifice of a child is the greedy god that society has created, and not the loving, comforting, omniscient deity to whom the hymn is composed.

The musical score does not always function ironically. In fact, the film's most hopeful scene is the recorder scene, where the score's lighter melody is inserted diegetically: Stefan and his girlfriend share a kitchen chair in a cramped apartment kitchen and are playing the recorder together. In this scene, we see a rare moment of human connection in an otherwise dystopic film—a connection made possible through the act of making music. "[Andersson] wanted to have some hope in the film," said Larsson, who played Stefan. "It needs to be there."[47] Music also connects people in the film through shared sorrow, functioning as collective human lament. The most powerful example of this occurs about fifteen minutes into the film, when subway commuters inexplicably break into a kind of elegiac aria (as I discuss in the coming chapter). Tellingly, the only person on the train who does not sing in the subway scene is Kalle, who—although he stands facing the camera—avoids meeting its gaze and clings to a pole, clutching a dirty hanky. This is the scene that introduces us to Kalle, and as we subsequently learn, not only does he fail to apprehend the healing power of the arts, he also fails to connect with the people in his life, is haunted by his debts and his failures, and is mired in self-pity. Andersson poses a strong contrast between Kalle and his son Stefan, who seems to be one of the only people in the film who hasn't ceased to care about others. There is some hope to be found, the film suggests, in the younger generation.

Benny Andersson's score includes three different musical themes with variations. He presented them to Roy Andersson, who decided which themes to use where. "He has a very clear vision and knows exactly what he wants," Benny Andersson said in an interview published in the film's press materials (Triangelfilm 2000). In fact, there are many long moments—even entire scenes—in the film where there is no music. In those moments, long pauses, or even the total absence of dialogue, accentuate certain trivial diegetic sounds, giving them added significance. Some examples are the magician's heavy sigh as he sits on the edge of his bed the night he has wounded a man in his show and the creaking of the bed as his lover slowly turns away from him; Robert's noisy winding of a clock in the bedroom scene with Pelle; and the sounds of the perpetual traffic jam. Reinhold Zwick argues that such moments evoke the film's plaintive, repetitive score: "When Andersson acquaints us with the old men with their failed lives, burdened by fate's final blows as they sit on the edge of their beds, it suggests the sad refrain of the 'Songs'—lamentations and elegies that the film composes in pictures instead of notes" (2008,

99–100). Thus the film's refrain is present even when it is absent. "Together," Zwick writes, "these visual 'Songs' constitute a great polyphonic lament for a sinking society" (100).

Just as Roy Andersson works analogic repetition into the film's dialogue and the sequence of images, so he uses Benny Andersson's musical themes as leitmotifs with modest variations, even inserting them diegetically at times. For example, the Muzak-style horn theme that plays during the magician's nightclub act—which Roy Andersson said was by far the most challenging for the composer to write—is repeated later, as a kind of faint echo, in the scene near the end of the film when Stefan and his girlfriend visit Tomas in the asylum. As Stefan tries to convince his brother Tomas that people really do care about poetry—"they just pretend that they don't"—the dialogue is accented by the ambient noise of a perpetual traffic jam outside the open windows, blended with a stripped-down version of a single horn playing the same nightclub Muzak featured in the magician's failed show. While we don't see him, the horn music suggests there is a street musician down on the sidewalk who is attempting to earn coins from passersby and being drowned out by a cacophony of car horns. Through this leitmotif, the film connects two disparate scenes and three failed artists—a poet who has lost his voice, a magician who has lost his touch, and a musician who can hardly be heard. They are not connected through any plot or narrative, but rather through their shared humanity and their collective sorrow over an inability to make poetry, magic, or music happen.

4

Humanism: Film as Philosophy and Social Critique

While the trivialist aesthetic Andersson showcases in *Songs from the Second Floor* may have been new to moviegoers, the film's critiques were not—at least, not to Swedish viewers. As Daniel Brodén has argued, "It would not be overstating the case to claim that Andersson has devoted his entire artistic project to the interrogation of the human condition and the reification of social life in the Swedish welfare state," from his debut *A Swedish Love Story* (1970) to the "trilogy about being a human being" that *Songs* began (2014, 101). Indeed, since the 1970s, Andersson has cultivated his standing as a public intellectual in Sweden, unafraid to criticize not just the film and cultural establishments but also the political establishment, social institutions, and civil society. The two books he wrote and coedited in the 1990s could be described as testimonials for humanist engagement, and he has also voiced his views on cultural programs on Swedish television and radio and contributed many opinion pieces to Swedish periodicals. Some consist entirely of social critique, making no mention whatsoever of film.

From 2006 to 2009, Studio 24 helped craft a historical exhibition on Sweden and the Holocaust. The exhibition, which claimed that Sweden was a passive collaborator rather than a neutral neighbor during a twentieth-century genocide occurring right next door in Germany, was displayed at the Forum for Living History (Forum för Levande Historia) in Stockholm and traveled to museums around the country.[1]

Andersson's motivation to create art that seeks to unnerve viewers through depictions of philosophical and social problems is articulated in Finnish philosopher Georg Henrik von Wright's essay "Humanism as an Attitude to Life" (1978), which Andersson excerpts in his humanist anthology *Successful Freezing of Mr. Moro*: "Humanism's ideal of perfection is the educated person, who acknowledges the value of the truth over every authority. To seek the truth—in the form of artistic expression, scientific knowledge, or philosophical insight—is to develop our humanity" (Andersson, Boman, and Borbás 1997, 126, my translation). *Songs from the Second Floor* could be described as a dystopian view of what happens when we fail to develop our humanity by refusing to seek the truth and clinging instead to fate, or a similar higher power (in the world of the film, the Market) to revive a sinking society and save mankind. Paradoxically, it is truth and authenticity that Andersson strives for in a film characterized by abstractions, archetypes, and absurd and horrifying situations that distort reality. The omnipresence of human mortality pervades the film, which opens with a scene in a solarium where the tanning bed resembles an eerie postmodern coffin with a pair of human feet sticking out, and it concludes with a scene at the city dump that turns out to be a mass grave where the dead walk again. But Andersson believes such abstraction is necessary to illuminate what humanity's conditions truly are. As Reinhold Zwick has argued, "In [the images'] grotesque exaggeration, they have been distorted, not beyond recognition but rather so as to allow recognition of a process that has in actual fact been going on for some time" (2008, 103). *Songs* suggests that we have become so accustomed to the banal mechanisms of cruelty, exploitation, and apathy that they often fail to register or provoke a reaction. For Andersson, this failure to act is where the real horror lies.

The film's stunning images and its unconventional film language, however, often seemed to overshadow its humanist critiques in the critical reception of the film, both in Sweden and abroad. As scholar Charlotte Wiberg has argued, the film's sensational Cannes win in May 2000 (as well as Andersson's seductive comeback story) validated the film as "high art" and conditioned Swedish critics to praise it as such when it premiered in Sweden in October of that year (2006, 269). A film critic for Sweden's largest newspaper, *Dagens Nyheter*, for example, wrote in her highly favorable review that while she didn't really understand the film, she admired its artistry: "The events in and of themselves are perhaps not particularly significant. On the other hand, Roy Andersson's artistic articulation has an enigmatic and enduring power of suggestion and originality" (Af Geijerstam 2000). Andersson himself has said that he is disappointed that *Songs* has not sparked more social debate about the issues it raises. In interviews and press materials, Andersson has sought to explain how *Songs*' goal is not only to develop the language of film to its full potential but also to ask hard questions about how humanity can achieve its full potential in the modern world. He even arranged for a special viewing of the film in the Swedish Parliament in November 2000 and introduced the film by diagnosing the problem that the film presents: "We have no plans for how to build our society."[2] While the screening was attended mostly by civil service bureaucrats rather than elected officials, Britt Bohlin of the Social Democratic Party did attend the screening and declared to a journalist beforehand, "Everyone who is inspired by social progress and political work should see this film." Afterward, she said to the same journalist that she disagreed with Andersson's indictment of the worker's movement in the film, but said it nonetheless was "important to ask the question about where we are headed" as a society (Tidningarnas Telegrambyrå 2000). Bengt Göransson, a former Social Democratic politician who was also active in adult education and temperance efforts, said in a 2000 interview that he "did not think that the film is an attack on social democracy. It is a general critique of the prevailing public mood" (Granath 2000, 10).

But as Nordh, who played Kalle in the film, also points out, the film demands a certain degree of intellectual engagement, as well as an awareness about the world, for viewers to understand its critiques. "You have to think about it—it's no damned cowboy film, you know. You have to be a little socially knowledgeable about things in order to grasp what it's about," he said. "You have to listen to politics, you have to know a little about everything."[3] Andersson's own politics have hardly changed at all since the 1960s, when as a film school student he embraced the 1960s radical politics shared by a number of established Swedish directors at the time. This was the era that produced Stefan Jarl's classic documentary *They Call Us Hooligans* (*Dom kallar oss mods*, 1968), Vilgot Sjöman's docufictional films *I Am Curious Yellow* (*Jag är nyfiken gul*, 1967) and *I Am Curious Blue* (*Jag är nyfiken blå*, 1968), and Bo Widerberg's *Elvira Madigan* (1967), *Ådalen 31* (1969), and, a few years later, *Joe Hill* (1971, about the Swedish immigrant who became a famous labor agitator in America). But even after decades of earning his daily bread making advertising films, Andersson has not shed his 1960s radical views, much to the irritation of some in Sweden's cultural establishment (and to the admiration of others). "That is Roy's greatest asset, actually, that he is so consistent," his longtime production manager, Johan Carlsson, said in an interview. "But his message isn't exactly so simple that you can capture it in a sound bite."[4] The aim of this chapter, then, is to examine the humanist critiques at work in *Songs from the Second Floor* through the ideas of some of the thinkers whose work has most shaped Andersson's own world view, in particular Austrian-born Israeli-Jewish philosopher Martin Buber's writings on existential guilt and French sociologist Loïc Wacquant's writings on advanced urban marginalization in the new millennium. This chapter also explores Andersson's lifelong preoccupation with the Holocaust and how its legacy continues to haunt humanity in his films. And, of course, it considers Andersson's critiques of the once-celebrated Swedish social welfare state, whose viability is very much in question in this turn-of-the-millennium film.

Life Is a Marketplace

In 1996, Andersson told a Swedish film journalist that *Songs from the Second Floor* would address economic injustices and inequality, "How the human being today is totally governed by economic laws [rather than actual, political ones] and the dangers that lie in the 'collective retreat' from the People's Home." He also promised it would be "a provocation against the established society and 'the enormous fatigue and apathy' that exists among society's leaders" (Fors 1996, 12–13). While the latter can be understood as a critique specific to Sweden and its welfare state (as I discuss later in the chapter), Andersson intended the former as a universal critique of the heavy toll neoliberalist dogmas have taken on developed Western societies such as Sweden's. While the filmic environment is deliberately archetypal and nondescript, its title, *Songs from the Second Floor*, evokes a particularly urban social environment of multiunit dwellings (Kääpä 2014, 113). French sociologist Loïc Wacquant, whose ideas

Andersson references in *Our Time's Fear of Seriousness*, argues that the postmodern, postindustrial, post-Fordist urban societies of the new millennium have fostered far more than increased poverty and inequality. Rather, they have fundamentally changed the way people see themselves in their urban environments as well as how they perceive one another. Even desperately poor urban neighborhoods once fostered a sense of unity and belonging, Wacquant argues, a sense of community among residents who would support one another through hard times. But new, more sinister and entrenched forms of social stratification have caused those dwelling in miserable social spaces to disassociate themselves psychologically, including distancing themselves from the people around them. "The current reconfiguring of capitalism involves not only a vast reshuffling of firms, jobs, and people in space but a sea-change in the organization and experience of space itself," Wacquant writes in "The Rise of Advanced Marginality: Notes on Its Nature and Implications," published in *Acta Sociologica*, the official journal of the Scandinavian Sociological Association in 1996 (126).[5] Andersson renders this "sea change" visually in his creation of monochromatic, muted urban environments devoid of color and life. "The absence of plants, animals (apart from rats), and children (apart from the girl sacrificed at the end) results in a pervasive atmosphere of oppressive lifelessness," Zwick observes (2008, 101). He points out that the proliferation of typically Swedish nicknames among the characters ironically underscores the lack of community in the dystopic world of *Songs*—"Lasse" for Lars, "Pelle" for Per, "Uffe" for Ulf, and "Kalle" for Karl—that evoke spirited boy characters in works by the famous Swedish children's author Astrid Lindgren (best known internationally for her Pippi Longstocking books). As Zwick writes, "These names inevitably remind Swedish viewers of . . . unencumbered childhood days in Bullerby or of Seacrow Island. But the old friendships, suggested by the nicknames, no longer count: in these circumstances, no one is anyone's neighbor" (103).

In fact, Wacquant argues that people's frustration over being stuck in such urban environments can cause them to act out aggressively against those who share their space. "All too often," Wacquant has written, "the sense of social indignity can be deflected only by thrusting the stigma onto a faceless, diabolized Other—the downstairs neighbors, the foreign family dwelling in an adjacent building, the youths from across the street who 'do drugs,' or residents over on the next block whom one suspects of illegally drawing unemployment or welfare" (1996, 126). In *Songs*, this is exemplified in a scene in which a group of young men beat up an immigrant on the sidewalk while a row of commuters waiting for the bus across the street looks on, doing nothing to help him even after the attackers have gone and the immigrant lies yelling in pain, blood trickling from his prone form. Significantly, all of the characters in this scene—the immigrant, the young men who beat him up, and those waiting at the bus stop—are dressed in middle-class work clothes; none are coded as poor thugs from an urban ghetto. And the fact that they are equally stuck in this dystopia, where Lennart's workers are being laid off by the hundreds just inside the office building, becomes, tragically, not a cause for solidarity but for anger, hatred, and aggression. The immigrant had been looking for someone with the surname Svensson, an ironic reference to Swedes' nickname for an average Swedish person (the English equivalent might be "an average Joe"). But "Svensson" is nowhere to be found in this new, estranged dystopia, or rather, he has been replaced by angry young men who taunt the immigrant, "Can you speak more clearly?" Right before the attack, we see several youths pushing a broken-down car up the street, providing an absurd metaphor for the lack of social mobility, one reinforced by the perpetual traffic jam motif. "Wherever one looks, the dream of a 'mobile society' is dead," Zwick observes, and the people living here have become similarly immobilized, feeling hopeless and helpless to determine the direction of their lives (2008, 103). In *Our Time's Fear of Seriousness*, Andersson explicitly links the fear and hatred of immigrants and non-Western "others" in today's society with the Nazi ideology that motivated the Holocaust (a point I return to later in this chapter).

The character of Lennart (the reigning capitalist boss who, tellingly, has no boyish nickname) embodies the archetype of the plutocracy whose actions ostensibly have caused all of this misery. In the opening scene, "The Oracle in the Solarium," Lennart has summoned Pelle so that he can give him a pep talk about laying off at least a thousand workers. Lennart is tanning himself in anticipation of a trip to Barcelona later that afternoon, so Pelle comes to see him in the solarium. In this scene, all we can see of Lennart's body are his bare feet, since he lies inside a tanning bed. The surreal glow coming from inside the bed and surrounding his feet, coupled with his disembodied voice, lend Lennart a bizarrely supernatural aura, an effect enhanced when Lennart intones a loosely cited verse from the Biblical book of Ecclesiastes: "Everything has its time." (One cannot help but think of the master illusionist in L. Frank Baum's *The Wizard of Oz*, who turned out to be nothing but a little man hiding behind a screen.) In *Songs*, the capitalist boss has become a godlike figure in a society that places its blind faith in the market to solve all of its problems. But unlike the Christian formulation of a loving God, Lennart—and because he is an archetype, all capitalist bosses like him—does not see to his people's needs. Instead, he lays them off by the hundreds, creating a negative ripple effect in the economy and throwing people's lives into chaos. (Andersson had ample real-life examples to draw from here, including one from his hometown of Gothenburg. During the Asian financial crisis, which crippled demand in that region, the multinational Swedish auto maker Volvo, which is based in Gothenburg, announced the layoff of six thousand workers—more than 7 percent of its global workforce.[6]) As Lennart continues his sermon, he modifies the line of Scripture to "The steam engine had its time," evoking the Industrial Revolution (roughly 1760–1840), a time when massive industrial expansion led to overcrowded cities, dangerous factories, and the parallel formation of an urban underclass and new elite class of rich industrialists. "It is a new time, Pelle. You have to understand that," Lennart tells him. As Zwick has pointed out, "The epochal change welcomed as 'a new day and a new era' by Lennart and the small privileged class means the utter abyss for everyone else" (2008, 104). When Pelle says it would be a "catastrophe" for many people if the company shut down, Lennart snaps, "Should we take responsibility for that?" and reassures Pelle that when the catastrophe comes, they'll no longer be here, because "why stay where there is a ton of misery?"

Later in the film, in the airport departure hall, we hear Lennart continuing his pep talk to Pelle as they drag heavy carts with baggage across the floor. In this scene, "Everything has its time" is followed by "Misery has its time"—implying that misery, like the steam engine, occurs naturally and inevitably, rather than as the result of human actions. (This is, in a sense, an ironic juxtaposition of what Jenny Andersson claims is Swedes' common view of their welfare model, namely that it developed as the inevitable result of Scandinavian morality and ingenuity; 2009, 231.) Lennart urges Pelle to "hang on" and reassures him that in a few hundred meters, "We'll be free people! Free at last!" As Zwick astutely points out, "Lennart unashamedly cloaks his egoism in religious garb: in his blasphemous farewell sermon at the airport he envisions his own escape from responsibility as both an exodus and a redemptive act. Through his use of phrases such as 'free at last' and 'a new day is dawning,' Lennart invokes the spirit of Martin Luther King's 1963 'I Have a Dream' speech, although Lennart's hymn is to a boundless hedonism that no longer considers anything sacred" (2008, 104). In the next scene in Tomas's room in the mental hospital, the sound of an airplane can be heard from outside the window, suggesting that the plutocracy were successful in making their escape, mingling with the sounds of the traffic jam on the street below. This contrast of sounds highlights the fact that while the golf club–bearing class makes its escape by air, the rest of humanity is either stuck in an interminable traffic jam or trapped in the subway in the underbelly of a dying city.

Kalle is among those riding the subway when we see him for the first time in a scene that provides the most memorable "song" in *Songs from the Second Floor*. This scene, like the one with Stefan and girlfriend playing the flute, functions as a musical and visual counterpoint to the alienation and hopelessness in so many of the film's scenes. The music begins nondiegetically, as we hear a chorus singing faintly in the background, and Kalle, whom we see for the first time, stands in the center of the frame, his face and trench coat covered in ashes (see cover photo). We do not yet know that a fire burned out his furniture store (we find this out in the dialogue of the next scene); no explanation is given here for his ashen appearance. As the music slowly builds to a crescendo, the commuters—from the foreground to the deep background of the train car—all open their mouths in a common aria that sounds like an elegy, filled with longing: "Aaaaaaaaaa—" until the nondiegetic sound fills the space of the commuter train. The scene presents no significant event that inspires the commuters' lament; rather, it seems simply to stem from the daily grind of riding a dark, shaking train in the company of strangers en route to and from a long workday (a feeling to which many an urban commuter surely can relate). Because any reading of this scene as naturalistic fails utterly, we are left with a symbolic interpretation:

as the lament swells around him, Kalle appears to us as an archetype for a fallen humanity, the ashes denoting both his mortality and his guilt—which, as we shall see, haunts him throughout the film.

The human lament continues into the next scene in a city bar (see figure 2.4), where the bartender and a woman using the phone join in, and Stefan sits slumped silently at a nearby table, an empty glass in front of him. Andersson's use of both a graphic match (through the open, singing mouths of the bartender and the patron) and a sound bridge (through the lament) links the people and their shared sorrow in the two scenes. Furthermore, since the lament begins nondiegetically, as something presumably only the viewers can hear, and then moves into the diegetic space of the train car, the lament effectively pulls us into the film's spaces of shared humanity. Their/our lament concludes in the archetypal bar, where many, like Stefan, go to drink away their sorrows and others tell their troubles to a bartender, which Kalle proceeds to do once he enters the bar from the street. In the background, the noisy, interminable traffic jam is put on full display: just outside the bar's windows to the right, we see a clump of cars with their brake lights on, trying in vain to round the corner to where a seemingly endless stream of headlights (seen through another window on the left) extends into the deep background. As the musical lament falls silent, the female patron resumes her phone conversation, pleading with someone named Krister that she's stuck in traffic and hasn't advanced more than a few hundred meters in four hours. Moments later, when she turns to the others in the bar and asks, "Is there anyone who knows how we can get out of here?" the question lingers as both rhetorical and metaphorical. Everyone is stuck in this misery. The reason they cannot get out, the film suggests, is that they have no idea how they got there in the first place. And those who do know have denied culpability and flown away.

Wacquant's theory of advanced urban marginality builds on earlier work by British sociologist Dennis Smith, who has argued that the breakdown of community in urban neighborhoods "is also fostered by the tendency to retreat into the privatised household and by strengthening of feelings of vulnerability arising in the course of the pursuit of fulfillment or security" (Smith 1987, 297, as quoted in Wacquant 1996, 126). Such feelings of vulnerability are exemplified in Kalle's hilariously plaintive refrain in which he expresses longing for stability and security—two (allegedly unkept) promises of the Swedish welfare state—which he first makes to the bartender and the repeats in several subsequent scenes. When the bartender asks him how he's doing, Kalle responds, "What can I say? It's not easy being human," and she agrees with him, handing him a beer and pointing out that his son, Stefan, has been waiting for him for several hours.[7] After wailing that his store has burned down and he is ruined, his tone becomes softer and more philosophical when he speaks with his son. "I wanted to talk to you," Kalle says to his son. "About what?" his son replies. Kalle intones, "You know—the future. How everything's going to, be. What we're going to do. How we'll get by. How we're going to put a little food on the table and enjoy ourselves a bit." Nordh's portly bearing and broad southern accent code him as a simple country fellow who has lost his way in the big city, and his plaintive tone as he speaks these words underscores his vulnerability. Swedish film critic Carl-Johan Malmberg of *Svenska Dagbladet* described Kalle's character as "a plump Edvard Persson figure transformed into a monumental Job," and Håkan Lahger of *Film & TV* described him as "a people's home hero in shabby armor" (Malmberg 2000; Lahger 2000, 25). Kalle's anxiety becomes palpable in the next scene when he returns to his mistress's apartment and confesses that he set the fire; in an act of financial desperation, he hoped to collect insurance money for the torched inventory. "I'm afraid I'm going to be found out!" he wails, burying his sooty head in her unsympathetic lap.

Kalle's next business venture is one that puts him even more at the mercy of market forces: selling crucifixes, presumably on commission. The scene opens at a trade fair, where a sales manager, Uffe, holds up a wooden crucifix toward Rune, a business associate, and begins to quote loosely the Golden Rule from the New Testament gospel according to Matthew: "Do unto others—" and Rune finishes it for him "—as you would have them do unto you." Uffe perverts the Golden Rule, which is meant to teach kindness toward and respect for others, by using it to upbraid Rune, who has failed to meet his financial obligations. As Zwick observes, "The manner in which the 'golden rule' is appropriated here results in a degradation of its status to that of merely a 'marketing' slogan" (2008, 109). The crucifixes are Uffe's latest business idea; as he later explains to Kalle, "We're headed for the year 2000! And he [Jesus] is the one whose birthday it is. A chance like this only comes once in a lifetime. It will be another thousand years before this man is so important again." Behind Uffe stand three life-size crucifixes, a satirical allusion to the Passion story at Golgotha, where Jesus was crucified along with two convicted criminals. In the market-ruled society of *Songs*, Jesus has been emptied of his power to save humanity and become merely a millennial product. The nail on one of the crucifixes comes loose, causing its Jesus to swing back and forth from one hand, mimicking the motion of a clock pendulum, a further reference to human time and the approaching millennium. Uffe's assistant, scurrying to fix the defect, asks if anyone has seen the nails. "In an attempt to sacrifice him to the idol of 'the market,'" Zwick argues, "Jesus is crucified yet again on plastic crosses that are designed to celebrate the millennium but have already become disfigured at the trade fair" (106). Jesus's commodification makes him an undesirable product, since his capacity to save mankind is what gave him meaning and power—something Uffe misread, through his market-informed worldview, as mere trendiness. "How could I be so dumb, so stupid, to think that I could make money on a crucified loser!" he says to Kalle in the film's closing scene (see figure 4.4) as he tosses his unsold inventory of crucifixes onto a pile at the dump, whose crosslike pattern and its location outside the city evoke another Golgotha—one that extends as far as the eye can see.

Guilt toward Existence

The historical event of the Holocaust has haunted Andersson all his life and informs virtually all of his creative work. Perhaps the most shocking individual scenes evoking the Holocaust do not appear in *Songs* but rather in the two commissioned shorts Andersson made in the decades prior: *Something Has Happened* (1987), which features Nazi soldiers and scientists conducting deadly cold experiments on Jews,[8] and *World of Glory* (1991), which opens with dozens of naked people being gassed to death in the back of a cargo truck (see figure 4.1). Both films feature the amateur actor Klas-Gösta Olsson, who also has a memorable role as a military officer taking a taxi ride to a general's one hundredth birthday in *Songs* (as I'll discuss shortly). In *World of Glory*, Olsson plays a real estate agent giving viewers a banal account of his apparently very ordinary life. However, in the short film's opening scene—the only scene in which his presence remains unnarrated and unexplained—he stands in the foreground wearing a dark suit, his back to the camera, looking at the back of a cargo truck crammed with naked, shivering people. Dozens of other men and women, also wearing nondescript dark suits, stand silently watching as well, their cars and motorcycles parked in the background of the large vacant lot. A whimpering child clings to the ramp, and a portly man slams his foot against her hand to release her grip, closes and latches the doors, puts up the ramp, and attaches a hose from the truck's gas pipe into an opening in the cargo door. As screams are heard from inside the truck, Olsson's unnamed everyman character turns his head behind him and looks directly into the camera.

The scene illustrates Andersson's claim in *Our Time's Fear of Seriousness* that "the camera is nothing more than time and history looking." In *World of Glory*, when Olsson looks back into the camera at us, he makes all of us material witnesses—this time, to genocide. Andersson's goal in his short film, as well as in *Songs*, is to convince viewers that the moral and political conditions that led to the Holocaust have continued into the new millennium. "That is why the protagonist looks into the camera: he is looking at history, at memory, at time and at us," Andersson writes (2010, 278). Furthermore, Andersson believes, we cannot hope to reconcile with the horror of this past until we acknowledge our own moral culpability, which we all share simply by virtue of being human. Andersson has called such culpability "guilt toward existence" (*skuld mot existensen*), a concept he bases on Buber's articulation of existential guilt in the essay "Guilt and Guilt Feelings," originally published in the journal *Psychiatry* in 1957. In the essay, Buber argues that all of humanity is connected through human relations and acts, which means that the harm that comes from a single act creates a ripple effect across time and space. "Each man stands in an objective relationship to others," Buber writes. "The totality of this relationship constitutes his life as one that factually participates in the being of the world. It is this relationship, in fact, that first makes it at all possible for him to expand his environment [*Umwelt*] into a world [*Welt*]." Buber does articulate a path to reconciliation for the harm we do to others, one in which Andersson finds the

4.1 "Gas Car." Opening scene of the award-winning short film *World of Glory* (1990). Andersson re-creates a mobile gas chamber of the sort the Nazis used for mass killings before construction of the better-known chambers at concentration camps. Here, instead of soldiers, the perpetuators and witnesses of the genocide are all civilians in professional work clothes, and they look back into the camera at points. Photo courtesy of Studio 24; used with permission.

greatest hope for humanity "in his place and according to his capacity, in the given historical and biographical situations, to restore the order-of-being injured by him through the relation of an active devotion to the world—for the wounds of the order-of-being can be healed in infinitely many other places than those at which they were inflicted (Buber 1965, 136). According to this reasoning, while it is impossible to seek atonement from those who actually died in the Holocaust and similar atrocities, it is possible to acknowledge our complicity, in our own place and time, for human actions and situations that echo those of the Holocaust and seek atonement in our own place and time. Andersson has cited examples, such as the emergence of the neo-Nazi movement in Europe in the 1990s and the postmillennial presence of radical nationalist political parties in many European parliaments today, including Sweden's. "What beautiful comfort it was to read that formulation," Andersson said, "that you can become reconciled if you have experienced an existential guilt, that you can make things right by doing something good in another place and another time."[9]

In *Songs*, Andersson illustrates this point in a scene that leads up to the film's only flashback, connecting Kalle's present guilt not only to his own past actions but also to humanity's shared trauma of the Holocaust. Toward the end of the train station scene discussed in chapter 1, after the commuter's finger is released from the door, the crowd of people slowly disperses until only Kalle and another man remain on the platform. The man turns out to be Kalle's old friend Sven, who committed suicide before Kalle could repay him the money he owed him. In the only instance in the film in which the camera moves, a tracking shot shows Sven following Kalle down the platform, literally and visually dogging him with his guilt. Kalle stops, sets down his wrapped crucifix from the trade show, and greets Sven, who shows Kalle his bloodied wrists. His wounds resemble those made by nail holes, casting Sven symbolically as a Passion figure. A Russian teen wearing anachronistic garb and a noose hanging around his neck approaches them from the background, anxiously repeating phrases in Russian that Sven translates for Kalle. "He's lost," Sven said. "He's looking for his sister." Sven explains to Kalle that the teen had wronged his sister and hadn't had time to make it up to her before they both were hanged. Then a flashback reveals that the teen is indeed lost in time as well as space. In the flashback scene, a teenage girl is hanging by her neck, already dead, as the Russian teen is brought to the scaffold. The only sound in the scene is the

4.2 "The Scaffold in Minsk." Shot in April 1998. The previous year, Andersson's crew had attempted a more faithful reconstruction of a World War II photo that had haunted Andersson since childhood, but Andersson was unhappy with the result. This second staging is a free interpretation of the original photo: the soldier at the left of the frame is about to raise his camera to document the hanging as the Russian boy (Fredrik Sjögren) tries in vain to ask his dead sister for forgiveness. Photo courtesy of Studio 24; used with permission.

nondiegetic music of Benny Andersson's haunting film score; we see the teen's mouth moving as he tries in vain to communicate with his sister, but we cannot hear his pleas for forgiveness, just as his sister cannot.[10] As the noose is placed around the teen's neck, a soldier in the left of the camera frame raises his camera and takes a picture to document the execution (see figure 4.2).

This scene in the film, titled in the script "The Scaffold in Minsk," is a reconstruction of a famous historical photograph depicting the first public execution of members of the Russian resistance in Minsk on October 26, 1941 (see figure 4.3) The hanging victims were in fact not brother and sister but fellow resistance fighters, a fact of which Andersson eventually became aware, but he decided the sibling relationship worked better in the film script.[11] Masha Bruskina, a Jewish communist, was seventeen when she died, and Volodia Shcherbatsevich, the son of the resistance group's leaders, was sixteen (Tec and Weiss 1997, 366). Holocaust scholars Nechama Tec and Daniel Weiss have written that the public executions themselves were intended to intimidate the population. But when Andersson saw the photograph for the first time in one of his father's books on the Second World War, he wondered why anyone would take photographs documenting their crime against humanity for posterity. Indeed, Tec and Weiss write that the Lithuanian photographer's series of photos from that day "depict the execution in near clinical detail," from soldiers parading the condemned resistance fighters down the street to their bodies hanging on display for three days at the factory gate (368). The fact that the photographs were made public after the war, and that they've circulated widely in various publications, supports Buber's assertion that "we who are living today know in what measure we have become historically and biographically guilty. That is no feeling and no sum of feelings. It is, no matter how manifoldly concealed and denied, a real knowledge about a reality" (1965, 132). In other words, it is impossible for anyone living in the world today to profess ignorance of these atrocities. The question that remains is what we do with that knowledge.

In the re-created hanging scene in *Songs*, before soldiers can remove the block from under the boy's feet, the film cuts to a present-day scene in the train station café, where Sven and Kalle discuss the Russian teen's fate. Thus we do not witness the boy dying but apprehend the fact and the tragedy of it. Kalle confesses to Sven, "I was relieved

4.3 Photograph taken by a Lithuanian SS officer in October 1941 documenting the hanging of Masha Bruskina and Volodia Shcherbatsevich, two teenage members of an underground resistance movement in Minsk. Andersson was a child when he first saw this photo in a book owned by his father, who had served in the Swedish military during the war. Copyright German National Archives (Bundesarchiv); used with permission.

when I heard that you were dead. 'Now I don't have to pay back the money,' I thought. There was of course no documentation. I was free from my debt." This last line takes on a particular irony in Swedish, as the word for "debt," *skuld*, also means "guilt." Kalle may be free of his financial debt (*skuld*) to Sven, who died with no heirs, but his personal guilt (*skuld*) remains. Furthermore, Kalle is now haunted by an existential guilt for an inhumane act committed against a stranger in another time. Because the Russian teen cannot reconcile with his sister, he seeks help from Kalle. This existential guilt, in the form of the Russian teen, dogs Kalle even more persistently than that of his dead friend, following him home on the subway. Kalle turns and says, "You'll have to forgive me, but I cannot help you because I cannot understand what you are saying." But he knows what the teen is saying; Sven has already told him, and the teen repeats the same lines again and again. Reading Buber, we know that the real reason Kalle cannot help the teen is that he has not come to terms with his own guilt and thus is of little use to others. In the film's final moments, Sven, the Russian teen, and Anna, the sacrificed girl, haunt Kalle once again at the film's postmodern Golgotha, the dump outside the city where Kalle has just disposed of his crucifixes (see figure 4.4). Kalle picks up a rusty gasoline can from the junk heap and hurls it at them in frustration, wailing that his life is hard enough without them tormenting him. As it hits the ground, a thousand dead people leap up from the ground and scatter like field mice, then stop, turn, and join the other three in walking slowly toward Kalle, who now faces a human mass rather than three individuals. The sudden appearance of so many others evokes the mass unmarked graves of wars and genocide. Kalle's attempt to chase away his guilt only brought it forth en masse, underscoring the futility of such an effort. More importantly, this final scene strongly suggests that when we deny our shared humanity, past and present, we compound not only our guilt but also human suffering.

Andersson was born in the final years of the Second World War and has always been fascinated by tales he heard from his father, who fulfilled his compulsory military service at the Swedish border with Norway during the war. While Sweden was officially neutral, it did send its military to guard its borders. "We were so fascinated when he talked about how they saw the German soldiers on the other side of the river, and [my father] noticed also—he was of course a poor,

4.4 "At the Dump—The 1,000 Dead." Exterior shoot, September 1999 at Stora Alvaret, a limestone plain on the island of Öland, just off Sweden's southeastern coast. Kalle turns away from his dead stalkers: Anna, the sacrificed girl (Helene Mathiasson), Kalle's friend Sven (Sture Olsson), the hanged Russian boy (Fredrik Sjögren), and a thousand dead people who sprang up from the soil when Kalle tried to chase Sven away. The road, the dump, and the model of a city skyline in the background are all part of the set that the film crew built on the barren plain. Photo courtesy of Studio 24; used with permission.

simple person, so to speak, but he clearly noticed that the [Swedish] officers were extremely friendly toward the Germans."[12] Due to its official neutrality, maintained through careful diplomatic relations with Germany, Sweden was the only Nordic country to prosper economically both during and after the Second World War, since Denmark and Norway were occupied by the Nazis, Finland was defending itself against the Soviet Union in a series of wars, and Iceland was geographically isolated in the Norwegian Sea. Thus while most of Europe struggled to rebuild, Sweden's economy boomed. This grates on Andersson. "I hate that Sweden behaved so opportunistically during the war," he said in a 2008 interview (Clarke 2008, 36). Sweden's role in the war has been the subject of much popular and scholarly debate in recent years, with ample disagreement as to whether Sweden's leaders were overly friendly and accommodating toward the Nazis or whether their official neutrality allowed them to assist their Nordic neighbors behind the scenes.[13]

Two of *Songs*' scenes, both featuring the Swedish military, implicate Sweden in the Holocaust. The first features Olsson (the protagonist in *World of Glory*) as a military colonel who climbs into Stefan's taxi and asks to be taken to a care facility for rich elderly people, so that he can hand over the speech he has written in honor of a retired general's one hundredth birthday. He summarizes the speech for Stefan: "Life is a voyage, a journey," he says. "Our map and our compass, they are our traditions, our heritage, our history, don't you think? And if we don't understand that," he continues, "we'll soon end up in darkness." The officer's summarized speech replicates the language of the "Song of the Swiss Guards 1793" epigraph from Céline's novel *Journey to the End of the Night*, which Andersson used as an epigraph on his unsuccessful Swedish Film Institute (SFI) funding proposals. (This quotation is also stenciled on the wall above the piano on Studio 24's second floor). Céline clearly intended his novel's epigraph to be ironic, because in 1792, during the French Revolution, nearly all nine hundred of the Swiss Guards, an elite corps tasked with guarding the Pope and France's royal family, were massacred while protecting the Tuileries Palace in central Paris (Czouztornare 1992). Thus in 1793, the date of Céline's epigraph, the Swiss Guards would be singing and walking while dead—which would indeed explain the darkness, the cold, and the lack of direction. (The protagonist of Céline's novel, a soldier who narrates the nihilism of war, is on this kind of journey.) In *Songs*, the colonel's speech is delivered in full in the subsequent scene, which opens with hospital staff preparing for the regiment's visit. Before the officers arrive, the hospital staff speaks admiringly about the old general's wealth: he is a millionaire who owns more land than anyone else in Sweden, with eight lakes on his property. Then the general's guests arrive, and the admiral reads the speech the colonel had composed, congratulating the old general "as a person and as a human being and as a representative of the safeguarding of our country, our traditions, our distinctive character and our history." The old general replies, "Give my greetings to Goering!" referring to Hermann Goering, Hitler's deputy, indicating that the old general was, indeed, very friendly with the Nazi regime. Through the articulations of his enormous wealth, the film implies that he was one of those Swedes who allegedly profited greatly from Sweden's role in the wartime and postwar economy. During the regiment's trumpet salute to him, he raises his arm in a recognizable "Sieg Heil" gesture and commands repeatedly, "Hoist the flags!," ironically linking Sweden's own nationalist pride to the extreme and grotesque form of nationalism writ large—fascism—that fueled Germany's National Socialists.

Condemning the People's Home

While global viewers can appreciate *Songs* as a universal dystopia, Swedish viewers had long been primed to grasp the film's critiques of their social welfare state. As Brodén has argued, the filmmaker's "comeback coincided with a trend of nostalgia for the aesthetics and values of *Folkhemmet*—for example, both functionalist design and modern welfare state history have enjoyed a revival of attention in the national culture in recent years" (Brodén 2014,

127). But while politicians from all sides have sought to elevate and restore this ideal, Brodén writes, Andersson "has maintained that although it is still a beautiful social vision, it has been seriously corrupted" (127). Swedes' nickname for their welfare state, *folkhemmet*, translates as "the people's home" in English; Social Democratic leader Per Albin Hansson popularized the term in an iconic political speech in 1928 to describe a social welfare state that cares for its people from the cradle to the grave. The Swedish *ett folk* is a collective term that often connotes a nation of people bound by a common language, history, and heritage.[14] In *Songs*, Andersson rejects modern nationalist dogmas evoking a *folk* and posits instead the fundamental value of the singular human being (*människan* in Swedish) —and of humanity (*mänskligheten*), regardless of national affiliation.

Sweden is known for its welfare capitalism, a system built on cooperation between government and business, or a middle way between socialism and capitalism. As historian Hans Sjögren explains, "Corporatism, compromise thinking, consensual democracy, low corruption, high taxes and an egalitarian spirit are often associated with the Swedish type of welfare economy" (2008, 22). What distinguishes it from many other welfare models (e.g., the United States) is that welfare benefits are distributed to everyone rather than only to those who meet a needs test, which helps maintain public support for Sweden's comparatively higher levels of taxation. Examples of this include Sweden's universal health care, subsidized day care, generous parental leave, and tuition-free public education—even at the college level. No Swedish political party that hopes to gain seats in Parliament would seriously propose ending these benefits. Pietari Kääpä has argued that one must understand *Songs'* critique of the Swedish capitalist welfare state to understand its ideological positions. "In Andersson's dystopian world, laissez faire individualism and consensual democracy contradict one another," which makes the system break down, Kääpä explains. Thus the films in Andersson's humanist trilogy "work as metaphoric encapsulations of societal malformations" (2014, 112).

Songs is, in a sense, a darker articulation of the dystopian vision Andersson first presented to Swedish audiences in 1985 in a classic commercial for the Social Democratic Party titled *Why Should We Care About Each Other? (Varför ska vi bry oss om varandra?)*. Set against a gratingly upbeat musical track repeating "Mah mah mah mah" is a series of images of what happens when people in a society stop caring. A large man in a bar pushes patrons out of their chairs and sits down (only to be displaced by an even larger man); exposed workers stir a poisonous industrial substance while their bosses look on wearing full protective gear; nurses and teachers demand payment from children before treating them or feeding them; and busy commuters ignore a man who flails about on the ground trying to gather the spilled contents of his briefcase. Together, the images answer the question superimposed on the final frame, "Why Should We Care About Each Other?," with the party logo below it. Andersson, who has never belonged to a political party, saw the commercial as a chance to critique the neoliberal discourses of the Moderates, the bourgeois party that was poised to take over the government from the ruling Social Democrats if it won the upcoming election. As Dahlén, Forsman, and Viklund have argued, "The stylized exaggerations made it possible to exemplify in concrete terms—and accentuate—what the consequences of the Moderates and the business sector's propaganda for 'market solutions' and individualism would be" (1990, 42). The commercial—Andersson's own favorite, and the one he credits with facilitating the breakthrough of his abstract film language—remains a classic, still studied, discussed, and circulated globally via YouTube.

Between the airing of that 1985 commercial and *Songs'* release in 2000, Andersson continued to prime Swedish audiences, as well as industry elites, for similarly over-the-top critiques he would make in *Songs from the Second Floor*. During that time, the director made more than three hundred "one-shot" commercials for Swedish and other European markets that used dramatic irony to make their points. As Brodén notes, Andersson's prolific and distinctive work in advertising means "many Swedes are more familiar with his films than with Ingmar Bergman's" (Brodén 2014, 101).[15] These one-shot commercials lingered in the minds of many Swedes who saw *Songs from the Second Floor*. For example, when journalist Mattias Göransson saw the departure hall scene, he found "it is impossible . . . not to think of Roy's cult classic advertising film for pension savings—the one where executive after executive, and in the end also the flight crew, jump out of the airplane wearing parachutes, but leave the passengers behind." In fact, Andersson has said the departure hall scene was inspired by historical news photos from the Khmer Rouge's takeover of Phnom Penh in Cambodia in April 1975, when hordes of people sought in vain to join the American embassy's evacuation in advance of the oncoming army (Göransson 2000, 28). Nonetheless, in this case, the earlier commercial—which, as advertising does, had a simpler, clearer message—helped elucidate the considerably more enigmatic context of *Songs'* departure hall scene. The critic Jan-Olov Andersson has mentioned the filmmaker's advertising film for Lotto, the Swedish national lottery, which features Lucio Vucina (the amateur actor who plays the hapless magician in *Songs*) as a middle-age couch potato who misses hearing the lottery numbers when his elderly father unknowingly sits on the remote control (2000). Andersson's advertising films are sometimes described as "anti-commercials" since, as the director himself once put it, "there isn't a single damn product that a person can't do without. That's why it's just ridiculous to make commercials that take the product seriously" (Göransson 2000, 69). But Andersson insists that he does take seriously the people featured in the commercials, as well as the people watching them. Swedish viewers' longstanding affection for the droll "losers" Andersson features in his advertising films arguably conditioned viewers to perceive the film's characters sympathetically—a necessary precondition. If we don't care about the characters, a satire of their life conditions fails to bite.

Lars Nordh said he believed the critiques in the film most comprehensible to Swedes are those of the health care system and the church, whose mission is to care for society's most vulnerable: the sick, the wounded, the poor, the elderly, and those in despair. In fact, it was in part the film's portrayal of clergy and health care workers that provoked filmmaker Lukas Moodysson's vocal criticism of it. "It is unfair toward those who work in caregiving fields to portray them as people who just stand and hang around and are lazy," Moodysson said in a 2001 interview with the Swedish magazine *Trots Allt* (Edgar 2001). Until 2000, the Church of Sweden (Svenska kyrkan), which is Lutheran, was a taxpayer-supported state institution; it became a private concern for the first time the same year *Songs* was released. Andersson's critique of the church in the film can thus be read as a critique of the welfare state's caregiving function. If those who work for caregiving institutions become preoccupied with material concerns, the film implies, they are unfit to respond to others who come to them in a state of existential despair. In the film, after Kalle loses his temper while visiting his son and is thrown out of the mental hospital, he goes into a church and sits down heavily in the pew. The head pastor and his associate enter, and Kalle stands up, thanks the pastor for his time, and proceeds to give him an account of his troubles: his business has burned up and his son has lost his mind and cannot speak to him. He concludes, "I am in despair." "In despair?" the pastor responds. "Who isn't?" Rather than attempting to comfort Kalle, the pastor gives an account of his own troubles: he's been trying to sell his house for four years with no luck, and he'll likely end up losing at least 200,000 Swedish crowns on the sale. The associate pipes up, saying that he'd purchased a package vacation before the travel agency went bankrupt, so he's lost both the money and his vacation trip. As Zwick has noted, the clergymen's preoccupation with money and their desire to sell what they have and leave places them in the same category as the business executives who flee the misery they have wrought (2008, 103). The fact that the head pastor feels at the mercy of a fickle market rather than a loving God also reinforces the notion that neoliberalism has become Sweden's religious dogma for the new millennium.

Six of the film's forty-six scenes implicate the health care system, a critique that arguably would be transparent to global viewers as well, since Sweden's taxpayer-funded universal health care has often been cited in debates about health care reform elsewhere, including the United States. Prior to *Songs*, Andersson had taken a direct interest in the health of Sweden's caregiving professions through the 1992 humanist anthology *Successful Freezing of Mr. Moro* that he coedited with Kalle Boman and István Borbás. The book was part of a campaign that the county government had contracted Studio 24 to carry out among its ninth graders.[16] Enrollment in schools that trained people for health care professions had been dropping dramatically, warning of a pending shortage of health care workers. Young people seemed more interested in better-paying professions, particularly in finance. "The prevailing yuppie mentality" in the schools, as Andersson calls it in *Our Time's Fear of Seriousness*, meant that "apathy toward 'the old, the sick, and those unfit for life' [*livsodugliga*] was widespread" (2009, 118). Stockholm County's Social Democratic government hoped that exposure to humanist texts and images and discussing existential questions would inspire more young people to choose caregiving professions. "[Health care] is a important sector of our society that depends on important questions about our birth, our health, and our death," Andersson writes in *Our Time's Fear of Seriousness*. "At its root are dimensions of a philosophical nature, which apply to our system of shared values, our understanding of the human being's worth and dignity" (2009, 120). The anthology's purpose was to foster humanistic thinking, and its method was to recuperate art and literature from an abstract and aesthetic domain and reanchor it in human experience. The book was distributed to a single grade of students throughout the Stockholm school system in 1992 (Pia Lundberg, now head of SFI's International Division, was among those who received one),[17] and Andersson claims that applications to health care programs doubled the following year (2009, 155). But one year into the campaign, as a recession loomed, a pro-business political alliance took over the county government and canceled the campaign, calling it incomprehensible and costly. Enrollment shortages in health care programs persisted, Andersson claimed, in spite of widespread unemployment among young people throughout the 1990s and tuition-free education (2009, 155).

In *Songs from the Second Floor*, two of the health care scenes take place in the emergency ward, where a doctor and a nurse seem too preoccupied with interpersonal conflicts to focus on patient care. Another such scene is the one in which the stabbed immigrant lies on a bed in the overcrowded hospital corridor; three others take place in the asylum where Tomas is confined. Nordh said the asylum scenes could easily be understood by Swedes as a critique of government reforms concerning psychiatric care, which were making headlines in the 1990s.[18] At the time, the recession caused the business-minded Stockholm county government to reconsider the high cost of housing mental patients at the infamous Beckomberga Hospital on

Stockholm's west side, which had opened in 1932 and by the mid-twentieth century had become Europe's largest mental asylum, with more than two thousand patients (Hyltén-Cavallius, Larsson, and Lihammer 2013, 37–38).[19] In 1995, the county government decided to phase out inpatient psychiatric care (a process completed in 1997) by capitalizing on new drug therapies that allegedly made it possible for mental patients to live independently and visit their psychiatrists' offices for treatment.[20] At the time, many worried about mentally ill people living among the general population.[21] In the asylum scenes in *Songs from the Second Floor*, we never see hospital personnel actually caring for patients; in fact, they are largely absent from these scenes. We see them only when a doctor comes looking for his lab coat and wrongly accuses a patient of taking his wallet, and when orderlies show up to take hold of a yelling Kalle and drag him out of the building. The only person who does actively care for Tomas is his brother Stefan. It's clear from these scenes that neither Tomas nor Kalle are getting the help they need from the social institutions that are tasked with providing it. (The rich, elderly centurion in the private nursing home, however, enjoys a whole cadre of doting staff.) In the world of the film, the People's Home is neither cozy nor secure, and the film's ample scenes in private home spaces are similarly cold and uncaring. In scene after scene, we see couples turning away from one another in bed or failing to soothe one another's pain. Stefan Larsson, who plays Stefan, said that Andersson's dystopic vision gives us a clear sense of what the world would be like if people cease to value, respect, and care for one another. "One must guard it all the time, humanism," Larsson said. "Otherwise, society can become a very cold place."[22]

Epilogue: Songs Carried On

The filming of *Songs from the Second Floor*, from the first scene to the last, took four years in a domestic film market in which a standard feature production lasts thirty days.[1] As Andersson has put it, "The most important trait of a filmmaker with ambition is patience" (Majsa 2015, 17). If Andersson had any doubts along the way, he didn't express them on set. In fact, those who have worked with him say that the secret to his success is his unflagging enthusiasm, which is infectious. "Roy has a lot of self-confidence, kind of like a soccer team coach," said Stefan Larsson, who—along with Lars Nordh—was involved in the film the entire four years. "He pushes people: 'Oh, we are going to make film history! This is going to be the best ever!' And, of course, I thought, 'Yeah, yeah, you have to take this with a grain of salt.' But somehow it still stuck."[2] Despite the long production schedule, Andersson's team was still working until the last minute to get the final cut of the film ready for screening at the Cannes Film Festival in May 2000. The film was originally scheduled to be screened early in the festival schedule, but due to its late arrival, it was screened on the last day instead. The expectations of Andersson's young and energetic crew were so high that they were actually downcast when it was announced that *Songs* had won the Jury Prize—the festival's second-highest award—rather than the Palme d'Or, which went to Danish director Lars von Trier for *Dancer in the Dark* (Göransson 2000, 106). Despite the director's twenty-five-year absence from feature filmmaking, von Trier had said that Andersson was the only competitor he feared (Romney 2001). "The distributors said they needed two days to think about the film," Lisa Alwert said at the festival after the prizes were announced. "Maybe it was dumb that it premiered on the last day" (Göransson 2000, 106). The Cannes win, however, not only restored Andersson's reputation as a feature filmmaker at home but also made it possible for Philippe Bober, Studio 24's international coproducer, to sell distribution rights to forty different countries, including the United States.[3]

Studio 24 made the Cannes Film Festival, which takes place in May, its target premiere venue and date for the subsequent films in the trilogy, which have appeared every seven years. *You, the Living* (2007) was screened in the festival's Un Certain Regard section and was nominated for, but failed to win, its top award. (It later won the Nordic Council Film Prize.) In 2014, the Cannes Film Festival committee declined to accept *A Pigeon Sat on a Branch Reflecting on Existence* for screening at the festival, a decision that sent shock waves through the Swedish film establishment and deeply disappointed Andersson and his crew. Ruben Östlund's film *Force Majeure* (2014) was accepted for Cannes's Un Certain Regard section and went on to win its Jury Prize, setting up a friendly competition between Andersson and Östlund at Sweden's national film awards the following January (see Lindqvist 2016). Andersson said later that he had needed more time to prepare *A Pigeon* for its premiere, as it was the first film in the trilogy shot digitally and the first using green screens in certain shots, so there was more postproduction work involved. One of the scenes shot with a green screen features colonial soldiers and barking German shepherds forcing chained African slaves into an enormous copper drum, then setting it on fire. In the scene featuring King Charles XII and his cavalry stopping at a bar en route to battle, Andersson used a digital technique to prolong the procession of horses so that the twenty animals brought into the studio for the shoot would seem like hundreds (Evry 2015). When the film went on to win the Golden Lion at the Venice Film Festival in September 2014, it was the first Swedish film ever to be so honored (Bergman was awarded a Career Golden Lion in 1971).

A Pigeon, like *You, the Living*, both stands alone as its own film and bears echoes of *Songs from the Second Floor*. A preliminary list of scenes for the first film in the trilogy includes one titled "The Seller of Novelty Articles," which did not make it into *Songs* but became a dominant motif in *A Pigeon*.[4] Also appearing on this list, but not in the finished film, is a sequence of seven (presumably short) scenes in which different characters are either playing a melody on a flute or moving their bodies in some way to the flute's music, with the melody presumably functioning as a sound bridge across scenes. While snippets of this did end up in *Songs* (albeit with a recorder instead of a flute), Andersson took time to develop these musical scenes more fully in the subsequent two films. While all of the films contain challenging scenes of human failure and human cruelty, the musical scenes in the second and third films in the trilogy infuse them with a levity that *Songs* lacks. In *You, the Living*, for example, droll, middle-age tuba players from the "Louisiana Brass Band" toot an upbeat tempo that becomes part of the film's score. The film's most ambitious scene is one in which a young woman named Anna dreams that she marries Micke, the lead guitarist in a rock band called The Black Devils, who has Gene Simmons hair, wears a tuxedo, and strums a tune on his electric guitar at the breakfast table while their apartment—which is in a train car—passes through the Swedish countryside and pulls into a station. "It was so nice. So very nice," Anna says wistfully as she recalls the dream. Andersson had had this scene in his head for years and had tried to include it in *Songs from the Second Floor*, but the crew was unable to get the mechanics to work, István Borbás said in an interview after *A Pigeon*'s release (Majsa 2015, 16). *A Pigeon* features a robust call-and-response musical scene in which the matron of "Limping Lotta's Bar" in Gothenburg promises shots of liquor to a regiment of soldiers who agree to pay her in kisses rather than cash during the wartime 1940s. Thus the first film in the trilogy—the only one that has the word "songs" in its title—actually passed along most of its musical scenes to the next two films. In his early conceptual sketches for *Songs from the Second Floor*, Andersson also included a Don Quixote and Sancho Panza–like duo, an element that did not make it into the first film but ultimately took form in the characters of traveling salesmen Sam (Nils Westblom) and Jonathan (Holger Andersson) in *A Pigeon* fourteen years later.[5]

In the two and a half decades since *Songs* premiered, Andersson's star has risen considerably in film markets beyond Western Europe. For example, *A Pigeon*'s American distributor, Magnolia Pictures, orchestrated an impressive rollout for the film's US premiere in June 2015, arranging for global auteurs Darren Aronofsky and Alejandro González Iñárritu to introduce Roy Andersson personally at its opening night screening in New York and including their endorsements in printed and digital marketing materials. National Public Radio aired a profile of the director on its *Weekend Edition* cultural program on June 6, and Andersson spent much of 2015 granting interviews to film journalists and cinephiles, with profiles on him appearing in publications ranging from the *Independent* to the University of California Berkeley's *Film Quarterly* (Ulaby 2015; Aftab 2015; and Ratner 2015). *A Pigeon* also returned Andersson to the Oscar competition for Best Foreign Language Film for the first time since *Songs*, with the Swedish Film Institute selecting his film as Sweden's entry for the competition in large part based on the successful marketing campaign Magnolia Pictures has carried out in the US market. New and old fans of Andersson's films need not fear that *A Pigeon* is his last installment, however. While Andersson initially conceived of *A Pigeon* as the culmination of a trilogy, at the Venice Film Festival in 2014 Andersson told Swedish film journalists that he still had so many unused ideas that he wanted to add a fourth film to the series (Tidningarnas Telegrambyrå 2014). In September 2015, he announced that he had begun work on a new film, tentatively titled *Of the Infinite* (*Om det oändliga*) (Bergqvist and Brander 2015). As *Indiewire* film critic Jessica Kiang wrote in her Venice Film Festival review of *A Pigeon*, "Unlike stupid real Christmas, cinephile Christmas only comes every eight years or so. That's how long it's taken Swedish legend Roy Andersson to mount each of the films in his 'trilogy about being a human being'" (2014). Given that Andersson managed to remain a major figure in European cinema without making a single feature film for twenty-five years leading up to *Songs*, the seven-year spacing of his ambitious, "high art" films since the turn of the millennium seems comparatively reasonable and regular. Andersson's enduring impact on the language and practice of the film medium cannot yet be fully measured, but one thing is clear. His "songs" carry on.

Appendix: Roy Andersson's Eclectic Oeuvre

Filmography

FEATURE FILMS

A Pigeon Sat on a Branch Reflecting on Existence (*En duva satt på en gren och funderade på tillvaron*, 2014)*

You, the Living (*Du levande*, 2007)*

Songs from the Second Floor (*Sånger från andra våningen*, 2000)*

Giliap (1975)

A Swedish Love Story (*En kärlekshistoria*, 1970)

*These three films comprise Andersson's "Trilogy about being a human being."

COMMISSIONED SHORT FILMS

World of Glory (*Härlig är jorden*, 1991). Commissioned by the Gothenburg International Film Festival and the Swedish Film Institute for the project "90 minuter 90-tal" [90 minutes of the '90s]. 15 minutes.

Something Has Happened (*Någonting har hänt*, 1987). Commissioned by the Swedish National Board of Health and Welfare, which blocked its completion. 24 minutes.

STUDENT FILMS

Besöka sin son [Visiting one's son, 1967]. 9 minutes.

Hämta en cykel [To fetch a bike, 1967]. 17 minutes.

Lördagen den 5/10 [Saturday October 5th, 1968]. 48 minutes.

DOCUMENTARIES

Den vita sporten [The white sport, 1968]. Cinematography by Andersson. Directed and produced by Grupp 13, a group of 1960s activist filmmakers including Andersson, Kalle Boman, Bo Widerberg, Lena Ewert, Staffan Hedqvist, Axel R.-Lohmann, Lennart Malmer, Jörgen Persson, Ingela Romare, Inge Roos, Sven Fahlén, Björn Öberg, and Rudi Spee. 102 minutes.

INFOMERCIALS

Tryggare kan ingen vara [No one can be safer, 1980]. Produced for Trygg-Hansa. 24 minutes.

Så fruktansvärt onödigt: Känslor och tankar kring barn och olyckor [So terribly unnecessary: Feelings and thoughts about children and accidents, 1979]. Produced for Trygg-Hansa. 57 minutes.

ADVERTISING FILMS†

"Styckare" [Butchers, 1987]. Produced for LO (Landsorganisationen i Sverige), the largest umbrella labor organization in Sweden.

"Lokföraren" [The engine driver, 1986]. Produced for Lotto [National Lottery].

"Spjälsängen" [The crib, 1985]. Produced for HSB today Sweden's largest housing cooperative, with its historical roots in 1920s early welfare-state housing reforms.

"Familjen" [The family, 1985]. Produced for Lotto.

"Varför ska vi bry oss om varandra?" [Why should we care about each other?, 1985]. Produced for Socialdemokraterna (Social Democratic Party).

"Lanthandeln" [The country store, 1985]. Produced for Sockerbolaget, the sugar company.

"Skrattande mannen" [Laughing man, 1985]. Produced for Televerket, a telecommunications company.

"Tullen" [The toll booth, 1982]. Produced for Estrella peanuts.

"Andjakt i vassen" [Duck hunting in the reeds, 1981]. Produced for Fazer candy company.

"Flamberingen" [The flambé, 1980]. Produced for Trygg-Hansa.

"Raggaren" [The joyrider, 1979]. Produced for Trygg-Hansa.

"Isvaken" [The hole in the ice, 1977]. Produced for Trygg-Hansa.

"Kajen" [The quay, 1976]. Produced for Trygg-Hansa.

"Glasrutan" [The sheet of glass, 1976]. Produced for Trygg-Hansa.

† This is an abbreviated list. Andersson has written, directed and produced more than three hundred advertising films, many of which have won international prizes. The list above includes some of Andersson's most iconic advertising films that have aired in Sweden and appear in the Swedish Film Institute's online database. Among the director's international clients are the dairy company Arla's subsidiary in Finland, Air France, and the carmaker Citroën. Many of Andersson's commercials, such as those for Felix ketchup, have aired in multiple markets. A sampling of Andersson's commercials can be viewed on the Studio 24 website at http://www.royandersson.com/eng/production/commercials.

Other Works

BOOKS

Vår tids rädsla för allvar [Our time's fear of seriousness]. 1st ed. Göteborg: Filmkonst, 1995; Rev. ed. Stockholm: Studio 24 Distribution, 2009. While this book is available in Swedish only, an excerpt translated into English titled "The Complex Image" was published in *Swedish Film: An Introduction and Reader*, edited by Mariah Larsson and Anders Marklund (Lund: Nordic Academic Press, 2010, 274–78).

Lyckad nedfrysning av Herr Moro [Successful freezing of Mr. Moro]. First printing, Stockholm: Gidlund, 1992; 2nd, 3rd, and 4th printing, Stockholm: Ordfront, 1997; 5th and 6th printing, Stockholm: Fälth & Hässler, 1999. This book, commissioned funded by Kultur- och utbildningsnämnden, Stockholms läns landsting [The culture and education committee of the Stockholm County Council], is out of print.

EXHIBITIONS

Vad roligt att höra att ni har det bra [How nice to hear that you're doing well]. Gävle Konstcentrum [Gävle Arts Center], 2015.

Sverige och Förintelsen [Sweden and the Holocaust], in collaboration with Kalle Boman and Stig-Åke Nilsson, at the Forum för levande historia [Forum for Living History] in Stockholm, 2006–9.

FILMS ABOUT ROY ANDERSSON'S FILMMAKING

Nilsson, Stig-Åke, Kicki Rundgren, and Kristoffer Sannestam. *För Holger i tiden* [For Holger in time, 2012]. Holger is the main character in Andersson's famous Felix ketchup commercials. 50 minutes.

Augustsén, Jonas Selberg. *Rum 1112* [Room 1112, 2012]. In Room 1112 at the Riverton Hotel during the 2011 Gothenburg Film Festival, Augustsén interviews a group of Sweden's most famous filmmakers, including Andersson. Inspired by Wim Wenders's documentary *Chambre 666* [Room 666, 1982]. 90 minutes.

Carlsson, Johan. *Tomorrow Is Another Day (Det är en dag imorgon också*, 2011). Carlsson, Andersson's longtime production manager, documents the making of *You, the Living*, showcasing Studio 24's unique filmmaking methods. This film had its world premiere in 2009 at the Museum of Modern Art's "Filmmaker in Focus" retrospective devoted to Andersson's work. It has since been screened at other international venues featuring Andersson's work, broadcast on Swedish television, and released on DVD. 90 minutes.

Arte, Per. *Lev människa . . . för helvete . . . så länge du kan!* [Live, human . . . damn it . . . as long as you can!, 2011]. This documentary also features the making of *You, the Living*, from its earliest stages to its premiere at the Cannes Film Festival, and includes Andersson's political views. 59 minutes.

Adams, Joséphine. *På genomresa—En intervju med Roy Andersson* [Walking through—An interview with Roy Andersson, 2009]. 9 minutes.

Smith, Dean. *Studio 24* (2003). This film documents the emergence of Roy Andersson's unique film production studio, Studio 24, in Stockholm. 57 minutes.

Andersson, Kjell, and Bo Harringer. *Den lilla människans storhet: Om Roy Andersson och hans film* Sånger från andra våningen [The greatness of the small person: On Roy Andersson and his film *Songs from the Second Floor*, 2000]. This film, codirected by Andersson's brother Kjell, documents the making of *Songs*.

Runge, Björn, and Ulf Brantås. "Dokument rörande filmregissören Roy Andersson" [Documents relating to the film director Roy Andersson]. Part Three of *Eldsjälar: En dokumentärserie i fem delar* [Driving forces: A documentary series in five parts, 1997].

Awards and Accolades (abbreviated list)

European Film Awards in Berlin, 2015, *A Pigeon Sat on a Branch Reflecting on Existence*

    Best European Comedy

European Film Festival in Palic, Vojvodina, Serbia, 2015

    The Aleksandar Lifka Award for extraordinary contributions to European film

Guldbagge Awards (National Swedish film awards) 2015, *A Pigeon Sat on a Branch Reflecting on Existence*

    Best Set Design, Isabel Sjöstrand, Julia Tegström, Sandra Parment, Ulf Jonsson, and Nicklas Nilsson

Venice Film Festival, 2014, *A Pigeon Sat on a Branch Reflecting on Existence*

    Golden Lion

Stockholm Film Festival, 2014

    Visionary Award

Jan Myrdal Society, Sweden, 2010

    Lenin Prize

Museum of Modern Art in New York, 2009

    "Filmmaker in Focus" retrospective

Fantasporto International Film Festival, Portugal, 2008, *You, the Living*

    Director's Week Award

Guldbagge Awards, 2008, *You, the Living*

    Best Film

    Best Direction

    Best Screenplay

Nordic Council, Copenhagen, 2008, *You, the Living*
    Nordic Council's Film Prize
Neuchâtel International Fantastic Film Festival, Switzerland, 2007, *You, the Living*
    Narcisse Award, Best Feature Film
Titra Film Award for *You, the Living*
Bodil Awards, Denmark's National Association of Film Critics, 2002
    Best Non-American Film, *Songs from the Second Floor*
Guldbagge Awards 2001, *Songs from the Second Floor*
    Best Film
    Best Direction
    Best Screenplay
    Best Cinematography, István Borbás and Jesper Klevenås
    Best Achievement in Sound, Jan Alvermark
Cannes International Film Festival, 2000, *Songs from the Second Floor*
    Jury Prize shared with *Blackboards* (*Takhté siah*), directed by Samira Makhmalbaf; Nominated for the Palme d'Or
University of Gothenburg, Sweden, 2000
    Hedersdoktor (honorary doctorate)
Stig Dagerman Society and Älvkarleby municipality, Sweden, 2000
    Stig Dagerman Prize
Norwegian International Film Festival, 2000, *Songs from the Second Floor*
    Norwegian Film Critics' Award
Uppsala International Short Film Festival, Sweden, 2000
    Uppland Film Trust Award

Odense International Film Festival, Denmark, 1993, *World of Glory*
  First Prize

Hamburg Short Film Festival, 1993, *World of Glory*
  Special Jury Prize

Montecatini International Short Film Festival, Italy, 1993, *Something Has Happened*
  First Prize

Clermont-Ferrand International Short Film Festival, France, 1993, *Something Has Happened*
  Press Award
  Special Jury Award

Montecatini (Italy) International Short Film Festival, 1993, *World of Glory*
  Best Film

Tampere (Finland) International Short Film Festival, 1992, *World of Glory*
  Best Fiction Film, International Competition

Berlin International Film Festival, 1970, *A Swedish Love Story*
  Interfilm Award
  UNICRIT Award
  IWG Golden Plaque
  Journalists' Special Award
  Nominated for the Golden Bear, which wasn't awarded that year due to boycotts

Andersson has also won numerous awards, both at home and internationally, for his advertising films.

Notes

Introduction

1. "G" likely refers to Gunnar Bergdahl, director of the influential Gothenburg Film Festival and a longtime colleague of Andersson's who also wrote the original foreword for *Our Time's Fear of Seriousness (Vår tids rädsla för allvar)*, first published in the festival's official publication *Filmkonst* in 1995. This translation and all subsequent translations from Swedish texts are my own, unless otherwise indicated.
2. The film won five Guldbagge Awards, for Best Film, Best Screenplay, Best Direction, Best Cinematography, and Best Editing. It was also named the 2000 Film of the Year by the Swedish Film Critics Society. The film was ultimately not chosen as one of the five official nominees for the Best Foreign Language Film Oscar, and Ang Lee's *Crouching Tiger, Hidden Dragon* (2000) won that year.
3. Roy Andersson, interview with the author, May 29, 2010.
4. Here again, Moodysson provides a notable exception, as I discuss in chapter 4.
5. For a detailed discussion of this influence, see Lindqvist, "The Art of Not Telling Stories," forthcoming in 2016.

6. Ruben Östlund, interview with the author, January 18, 2015.
7. "Veckans gäst—Roy Andersson," *Kulturprogrammet Sverige*, broadcast on Swedish television November 22, 2014.
8. "Han är filmvärldens Zlatan," *Kulturprogrammet Sverige*, broadcast on Swedish television on September 8, 2014. The title of the episode compares Andersson to a global superstar soccer player from Sweden, Zlatan Ibrahimović.
9. For an expanded discussion of the "slow cinema" movement, see, for example, Jaffe 2014; de Luca and Jorge 2015; and Lindqvist 2016.
10. Östlund interview.
11. This figure is taken from "Faktisk Finansiering" (actual funding), a document provided to the author by Studio 24's producer, Pernilla Sandström, in a 2010 meeting. In contrast, one of the Bergman films Andersson admires, *The Silence* (*Tystnaden*, 1963), cost an estimated one million Swedish crowns (Koskinen 2010). The most expensive Nordic films made to date are the two *Arn* films (2007–8), transnational epics based on Swedish author Jan Guillou's best-selling novels, which media outlets reported cost 210 million Swedish crowns.
12. The film cost an estimated four million crowns to make.
13. Andersson was awarded the Stig Dagerman Prize by the Stig Dagerman Literary Society in 2001, and the Lenin Prize by the Jan Myrdal Literary Society in 2010.
14. Roy Andersson, interview with the author, June 10, 2010.
15. This school, founded in 1963 as part of national film reforms, was replaced in 1970 by an institution independent of the Swedish Film Institute: the University College of Film, Radio, Television and Theatre in Stockholm. This institution has since merged with other arts schools to become part of the University of the Arts in Stockholm (Stockholms Dramatiska Högskola). See Söderbergh Widding 2016.
16. To be fair, Bergman did make successful comedies, of which the best known internationally is *Smiles of a Summer Night* (*Sommarnattens*

leende, 1955). The three Bergman films Andersson says he admires are also ironically among the darkest and most humorless of all of Bergman's films..

17. Aside from the two films mentioned, Widerberg's best-known films internationally are *Elvira Madigan* (1967) and his final film, *All Things Fair* (*Lust och fägring stor*, 1995).

Chapter 1

1. Andersson recounts this story in the director's commentary of the DVD released by New Yorker Video. He confirmed it in a May 29, 2010, interview with the author.
2. Kjell Andersson and Bo Harringer, *Den lilla människans storhet: Om Roy Andersson och hans film* Sånger från andra våningen (2000).
3. Östlund interview.
4. Roy Andersson interview, June 10, 2010.
5. Undated project description provided to the author by Studio 24.
6. Roy Andersson interview, June 10, 2010.
7. Roy Andersson interview, May 29, 2010.
8. *Songs from the Second Floor*, director's commentary.
9. World Economic Forum, *Global Gender Gap Report 2014*, accessed June 20, 2015, http://reports.weforum.org/global-gender-gap-report-2014/economies/#economy=SWE.
10. Roy Andersson interview, June 10, 2010.
11. Lars Nordh, interview with the author, June 4, 2010.
12. The film's official production notes list Alwert as "producer." Alwert said in an interview that Andersson, at Boman's urging, determined that this was the only fitting title for her, since she was the "go-to" person at the studio for so many aspects of the film's production, from logistical arrangements to finances to serving as Andersson's liaison to news media.

13. Lisa Alwert, interview with the author, June 10, 2010.
14. "Filmmakers Live: Roy Andersson & Ruben Östlund," Filmfest Munich, 2011, YouTube, accessed July 28, 2015, https://www.youtube.com/watch?v=nsCUTII3aT4.
15. Ibid.
16. Andersson 2010.
17. The third film in Andersson's trilogy, *A Pigeon Sat on a Branch Reflecting on Existence*, is inspired by the painting *Hunters in the Snow (Jagers in de Sneeuw*, 1565) by Flemish painter Pieter Bruegel the Elder (1525–1569).
18. I have not timed all of the film's individual forty-six shots myself but rather am relying on the work of an excellent master's thesis by Jon Inge Faldalen at the University of Oslo in 2008.
19. *Songs from the Second Floor*, director's commentary.
20. Bergman titled his 1987 autobiography *The Magic Lantern (Lanterna magica)*.
21. For a thorough discussion of Andersson's relationship to modernism, see Yang 2012.

Chapter 2

1. I'll include the Swedish original here, as the wording is quite idiomatic: "Det gäller att kunna tala för sig—lägga ut texten så det blir resultat."
2. Roy Andersson interview, June 10, 2010.
3. Pia Lundberg, interview with the author, June 8, 2010.
4. "Un Certain Regard Rendez-vous—Turist by Ruben Östlund," Cannes International Film Festival website, May 18, 2014, http://www.festival-cannes.fr/en/article/60953.html.
5. Eva Stenfeldt, interview with the author, June 7, 2010.
6. Pernilla Sandström, interview with the author, May 29, 2010.
7. Johan Carlsson, interview with the author, June 8, 2010.
8. Stenfeldt interview.

9. Carlsson interview.
10. This project was Hungarian director András Surányi's 2000 film titled *Film . . .* based on Miklós Mészöly's novel.
11. István Borbás and Jesper Klevenås, joint interview with the author, May 29, 2010.
12. Stenfeldt interview.
13. Carlsson interview.
14. Ibid.
15. This early project description of *Songs* is on file in the Swedish Film Institute (hereafter referred to as SFI) library. It is undated, but Andersson said it was submitted in the early 1990s.
16. Alwert interview.
17. Ibid.
18. Carlsson interview.
19. Roy Andersson interview, June 10, 2010.
20. Borbás and Klevenås interview.
21. Ibid.
22. Sandström interview.
23. Undated project description on file in the SFI library.
24. For more information about how the *konsulent* system operates for the purpose of awarding film funding, see SFI's website, http://www.filminstitutet.se/sv/sok-stod/filminstitutets-stod/filmkonsulenter/ (accessed October 30, 2015).
25. Anna Sardelis, SFI analyst for strategic intelligence and statistics, email exchange with the author, January 20, 2015.
26. From "Faktisk Finansiering," a list of funding sources provided by Sandström to the author.
27. Carlsson interview.
28. Sandström interview.
29. Roy Andersson interview, May 29, 2010.
30. Sandström interview.
31. Prior to the 1990s, Andersson had tentatively titled his forthcoming feature film *Här kommer jag!* [Here I come!] (a title that even

appeared in news stories about the film under development),which was an allusion to the poem "A Cloud in Trousers" by Russian modernist Vladimir Mayakovsky. Roy Andersson interview, May 29, 2010.

32. Stefan Larsson, interview with the author, June 2, 2010.
33. A veteran actor, Carlsson went on to feature in a number of high-profile films, playing Lisbeth Salander's original guardian in David Fincher's remake of *The Girl with the Dragon Tattoo* (2011) and a veterinarian in Jan Troell's *The Last Sentence* (*Dom över död man*, 2012). His leading role in Jens Sjögren's 2011 film *Lycka till och ta hand om varandra* [Good luck and take care of one another] earned him a Best Actor nomination in the 2013 Swedish film awards.
34. Larsson interview.
35. Ibid.
36. Nordh interview.
37. Larsson interview.
38. Ibid.
39. Nordh played Officer Forsfält, a local cop who assisted Wallander in his investigation.
40. Stenfeldt interview.

Chapter 3

1. "Sånger från andra våningen," undated project description provided to the author by Lisa Alwert.
2. The Swedish text quoted in the proposal is as follows: "Vårt liv är en resa / genom natt och mörker / vår bana vi leta / på himlen där ingenting brinner. / (Schweiziska Gardets visa 1793)." The first two lines of this stanza are stenciled to the upper wall of Studio 24's second-floor common area, above the piano. The English translation cited here is by Ralph Manheim (Céline 2006).
3. Roy Andersson interview, June 10, 2010.

4. For scholarship exploring the intermediality of film and theater, see, for example, Sandberg 2006 and Chapple and Kattenbelt 2006.
5. Borbás and Klevenås interview.
6. From a letter Andersson wrote to SFI in 1993, as quoted in Göransson 2000, 27.
7. Admittedly, Andersson's favorite authors—particularly Vallejo and Céline, the latter of whom is often condemned by cultural elites for his anti-Semitism—are not likely to be part of such a cultural canon in Sweden, but it is fun to imagine that they might be, in the world of Andersson's film. All four authors—Vallejo, Céline, Strindberg, and Beckett—are cited in Studio 24's humanist anthology *Successful Freezing of Mr. Moro* (1992), which I discuss in chapter 4.
8. The retrospective was titled *Filmmaker in Focus: Roy Andersson* and ran September 10–18, 2009. See http://www.moma.org/visit/calendar/films/990.
9. Spigland 2010; Göransson 2000, 68.
10. Bazin 1967b, 56.
11. Bazin 1967d, 167.
12. See Benjamin 1968 and Adorno and Horkheimer 1972.
13. Roy Andersson interview, May 29, 2010.
14. Lundkvist (1906–1991) was an influential Swedish poet, critic, translator, and member of the Swedish Academy. He published about eighty books that have been translated into thirty languages, and is also known for translating Spanish and French poetry into Swedish. A number of the foreign poets whose work he translated, such as Pablo Neruda, subsequently won the Nobel Prize for Literature.
15. Peter Landelius, email exchange with the author, January 22, 2015.
16. Roy Andersson interview, June 10, 2010.
17. Roy Andersson interview, May 29, 2010.
18. Ibid.
19. Fans of Andersson's advertising work may grasp the insider joke at work here, as one of Andersson's better-known commercials was one he made for LO in 1981 titled *"LO—Arbete för alla"* [LO—work for all].

20. Roy Andersson interview, May 29, 2010.
21. "Sånger från andra våningen (en existentiell komedi). Idébeskrivning och synopsis." Undated project description provided to the author by Lisa Alwert.
22. This English translation from the film dialogue is my own, although I have consulted Eshleman's and Barcia's award-winning translation (Vallejo 1980). The dates Vallejo originally wrote his poems that were published posthumously, including this one, have been debated among scholars. Referencing a date that appears on the unpublished manuscript, Eshleman and Barcia claim the poem was completed on October 11, 1937, in Paris, following Vallejo's last visit to Spain and the front of the Spanish Civil War. It was first published in *Poemas humanos*, edited by Vallejo's wife, Georgette, in 1939, the year after Vallejo's death.
23. The Sermon on the Mount is found in chapter 5 of the gospel of according to Matthew.
24. For analyses of Vallejo's cinematic work, see Duffey 2003 and Oviedo Pérez de Tudela 2003.
25. According to Franco (1976), the play was tentatively called *Charlot contra Chaplin*.
26. Roy Andersson interview, June 10, 2010.
27. Nordh interview.
28. Roy Andersson interview, May 29, 2010.
29. The poem appears in a section of the poetry collection subtitled "Sermón de la Barbarie" [Sermon on Barbarism]. For a detailed analysis of the parallels between Andersson and Vallejo, see Lindqvist 2010.
30. Anne Karhio (2012, 33) makes this connection between Simberg and Auden.
31. Roy Andersson interview, May 29, 2010.
32. Roy Andersson interview, June 10, 2010.
33. As Karhio (2012) points out, museum officials were pleasantly surprised that the public would chose such an enigmatic painting over works that articulate Finnish national identity—for example,

paintings by Akseli Gallen-Kallela (1865–1931)—evoking Finland's national folk epic, folk life, or significant historical events.

34. Hanich examines four different types of "hidden dimensions" in Andersson's work. This one would qualify as "suggesting and imagining" (2014, 46).
35. Roy Andersson interview, May 29, 2010.
36. Alwert interview.
37. Roy Andersson interview, June 10, 2010.
38. Ibid.
39. With the rise of Nazism, painters of the New Objectivity movement, along with many other celebrated artists of German expressionism, had their work confiscated and placed on display at the infamous "Degenerate Art" exhibit in Munich in 1937. As the United States Holocaust Memorial Museum website attests, "The pieces were chaotically hung with accompanying criticism and derisive text, in order to clarify to the German people what type of art was considered unacceptable."
40. The scene's Swedish title, as written in the script, is "Eftertankens kranka blekhet," which functions as a fixed idiom in Swedish and has a far more poetic connotation—something like "the sickly pallor of remorse"—than the simple English word "misgivings" (which is also how Studio 24 translates the title in its English-language press materials).
41. From the Grand Hôtel website, accessed July 28, 2015, http://www.grandhotel.se/en/about-grand-hotel/history.
42. In Swedish, "Är det samma visa idag också?"
43. Roy Andersson interview, June 10, 2010.
44. Ibid.
45. Benny Andersson, email exchange with the author, July 1, 2010.
46. Ibid.
47. Larsson interview.

Chapter 4

1. For more information, in Swedish, about the exhibit, see www.royandersson.com/produktion/utstallning. The actions of the Nordic nations, including Sweden, leading up to and during the Second World War have received increasing attention in recent years. The war has become a popular framing device for Scandinavian crime fiction writers, and Jan Troell's 2012 biopic *The Last Sentence* profiled Gothenburg newspaper editor Torgny Segerstedt, who was known for his scathingly critical columns opposing the rise of Germany's National Socialists.
2. This practice is not uncommon; films considered to be of social or political importance are sometimes screened in the Swedish Parliament.
3. Nordh interview.
4. Carlsson interview.
5. Wacquant was the student of the late French sociologist Pierre Bourdieu, whose nondogmatic approach to social critique and the hegemonic impact of bourgeois tastes and values resonated with many Swedish leftists of Andersson's generation.
6. See "AB Volvo History," Funding Universe, http://www.fundinguniverse.com/company-histories/ab-volvo-history/, accessed January 15, 2015.
7. Andersson has acknowledged that the line "It's not easy being human" is a veiled reference to August Strindberg's classic symbolist drama *A Dream Play* (*Ett drömspel*, 1901), in which a daughter of the gods who descends to earth to observe the human condition exclaims, "Det är synd om människan!," which has been translated many ways but essentially means "Humans are to be pitied." Roy Andersson interview, June 10, 2010.
8. Andersson has been roundly criticized by some scholars and officials for his insistence, in his short film *Something Has Happened* and in published opinion pieces, that the HIV virus was created by scientists

conducting lab experiments rather than transmitted to humans by infected monkeys. This thesis was a major reason the Swedish National Board of Health and Welfare, which had commissioned the film, stopped it prior to its completion (see Christopth Andersson 2013).

9. Roy Andersson interview, June 10, 2010.
10. Borbás and Andersson initially considered using Austrian composer Joseph Haydn's famous anthem that accompanies the "Deutschlandlied," Germany's national anthem popularized by the Nazis, but decided this would be overly didactic; Borbás email exchange with the author, June 21, 2010.
11. Roy Andersson interview, June 10, 2010.
12. Roy Andersson interview, May 29, 2010. For nuanced analyses of Sweden's complicated relationship with Germany, see Witoszek and Trägårdh 2002.
13. For scholarly accounts of Sweden's actions during the Second World War, see Ekman, Åmark, and Toler 2003. For the framing of ongoing debates in Sweden and Denmark, see Zander 2003.
14. The Swedish word *folk* is very close to the German word *volk*, whose nationalist import became especially loaded when the National Socialists came to power in Germany in 1933.
15. Bergman also made commercials (a fact less known outside of his native Sweden), so this comparison ostensibly includes both filmmakers' complete bodies of work.
16. The campaign, which was not the first attempt to address declining enrollment in schools for caregiving fields, had a budget of seven million Swedish crowns and was to last three years. The book was meant as the culmination of many materials, including posters, a film, and newspaper ads (Roy Andersson 2009, 118–19). The book takes its title from an iconic 1975 photograph, *Mr. Moro Successfully Being Frozen in Cake of Ice* (Underwood Collection, Bettmann Archive, Museum of Modern Art, New York), which features an experiment in which a man was deep-frozen in a block of ice and freed from it alive (Andersson, Boman, and Borbás 1997, 282–83).

17. Lundberg interview.
18. Nordh interview.
19. The asylum was well known among Swedes; as one blogger writes in a historical overview, "The name was negatively loaded. 'You should sit in Beckis!' was an ordinary expression when you chewed someone out for saying something crazy" (Eriksson 2014, my translation).
20. The closed asylum was renovated and reopened in 2013 as a conventional hospital serving the Bromma area. See Karlsson 2013.
21. This debate came to a head in 2003, when Sweden's popular and globally respected secretary of state, Anna Lindh, was fatally stabbed in a downtown Stockholm department store by a young man with a six-year history of outpatient psychiatric treatment and aggressive behavior. Her killer is now confined to the Forensic Psychiatric Regional Clinic in Växjö (Letmark 2004).
22. Larsson interview.

Epilogue

1. Östlund interview.
2. Larsson interview.
3. Sandström interview.
4. The undated document listing the preliminary list of scenes for the first film in the trilogy is titled "Scener i långfilmen 'Sånger från andra våningen' (preliminär ordningsföljd)" [Scenes in the fiction film 'Songs from the Second Floor' (provisional order)] and was provided to the author by Roy Andersson.
5. Roy Andersson interview, June 10, 2010.

Bibliography

Research Interviews

Alwert, Lisa. 2010. Robert's Coffee, Stockholm, June 10.

Andersson, Benny. 2013. Email exchange with the author, June 20.

Andersson, Roy. 2010. Studio 24, Stockholm, May 29.

———. 2010. Studio 24, Stockholm, June 10.

Borbás, István. 2010. Email exchange with the author, June 21.

Borbás, István, and Jesper Klevenås. 2010. Studio 24, Stockholm, May 29.

Carlsson, Johan. 2010. Studio 24, Stockholm, June 8.

Landelius, Peter. 2015. Email exchange with the author, January 22.

Larsson, Stefan. 2010. Gunnarsons, Stockholm, June 2.

Lundberg, Pia. 2010. Swedish Film Institute, Stockholm, June 8.

Nordh, Lars. 2010. Ekenäs, Småland, Sweden, June 4.

Östlund, Ruben. 2015. Le Méridien Chambers Hotel, Minneapolis, January 18.

Sandström, Pernilla. 2010. Studio 24, Stockholm, May 29.

Sardelis, Anna. 2015. Email exchange with the author, January 20.

Stenfeldt, Eva. 2010. Gunnarsons, Stockholm, June 7.

Works Cited

"AB Volvo History." Volvo website. Accessed January 15, 2015. http://www.fundinguniverse.com/company-histories/ab-volvo-history/.

"A Classical Meeting Place." Grand Hôtel website. Accessed January 6, 2015. http://www.grandhotel.se/en/about-the-grand-hotel/history.

Adorno, Theodor, and Max Horkheimer. 1972. "The Culture Industry: Enlightenment as Mass Deception." In *Dialectic of Enlightenment*, 120–167. New York: Continuum.

Af Geijerstam, Eva. 2000. "En koral i moll till samtiden." *Dagens Nyheter*, October 6.

Aftab, Kaleem. 2015. "Film-maker Roy Andersson Interview: 'This Movie Will Make You Smarter.'" *The Independent*, April 12. http://www.independent.co.uk/arts-entertainment/films/features/filmmaker-roy-andersson-interview-this-movie-will-make-you-smarter-10170862.html.

Andersson, Christopth. 2013. "Skona skoleleverna från Stasis aidsmyt." *Expressen*, February 6. http://www.expressen.se/debatt/skona-skoleleverna-fran-stasis-aidsmyt/.

Andersson, Jan-Olov. 2000. "Vackert och omskakande." *Aftonbladet*, October 6.

Andersson, Jenny. 2009. "Nordic Nostalgia and Nordic Light: The Swedish Model as Utopia, 1930–2007." *Scandinavian Journal of History* 34 (3): 229–45.

Andersson, Kjell, and Bo Harringer. 2000. *Den lilla människans storhet: Om Roy Andersson och hans film* Sånger från andra våningen. Trollhättan, Sweden: Film i Väst.

Andersson, Roy. 1995. *Vår tids rädsla för allvar* [Our time's fear of seriousness]. Göteborg, Sweden: Filmkonst.

———. 2004. "Director's Commentary." *Songs from the Second Floor* DVD release, New Yorker Video.

———. 2009. *Vår tids rädsla för allvar* [Our time's fear of seriousness]. Rev. ed. Stockholm: Studio 24 Distribution.

———. 2010. "The Complex Image." In *Swedish Film: An Introduction and Reader*, edited by Mariah Larsson and Anders Marklund, 274–78. Translated by Anders Marklund. Lund: Nordic Academic Press.

Andersson, Roy, Kalle Boman, and István Borbás, eds. (1992) 1997. *Lyckad nedfrysning av Herr Moro* [Successful freezing of Mr. Moro]. 2nd. ed. Stockholm: Ordfront Förlag.

Asplund, Karl. 1957. *Nils Dardel I: Ungdomstiden, 1888–1921*. Stockholm: P. A. Norstedt & Söners Förlag.

Balázcs, Béla. 2009. "The Close-Up." In *Film Theory and Criticism: Introductory Readings*, edited by Leo Braudy and Marshall Cohen, 273–74. 7th ed. New York: Oxford University Press.

Bazin, André. 1967a. "The Evolution of the Language of Cinema." In *What Is Cinema?*, edited and translated by Hugh Gray, 23–40. Vol. 1. Berkeley: University of California Press.

———. 1967b. "In Defense of Mixed Cinema." In *What Is Cinema?*, 1:53–75.

———. 1967c. "Charlie Chaplin." In *What Is Cinema?*, 1:144–53.

———. 1967d. "Painting and Cinema." In *What Is Cinema?*, 1:164–69.

———. 1971. "De Sica: Metteur en Scène." In *What Is Cinema?*, edited and translated by Hugh Gray, 61–78. Vol. 2. Berkeley: University of California Press.

Bell, James. 2004. "Small Is Beautiful." *Sight & Sound* 14 (8): 76.

Benjamin, Walter. 1968. "The Work of Art in the Age of Mechanical

Reproduction." In *Illuminations*, edited by Hannah Arendt, 217–52. New York: Harcourt, Brace & World.

Bergman, Ingmar. 2007. *The Magic Lantern*, translated by Joan Tate. Chicago: University of Chicago Press.

Bergqvist, Mattias and Maria Brander. 2015. "Roy Anderssons film Sveriges Oscarbidrag." In *Expressen*, September 1. http://www.expressen.se/noje/roy-anderssons-film-sveriges-oscarbidrag/.

Bibel 2000 med hittlistan. 1999. Göteborg, Sweden: Bokförlaget Cordia.

Bordwell, David. 2005. *Figures Traced in Light: On Cinematic Staging.* Berkeley: University of California Press.

———. 2007. "Vancouver Visions." *David Bordwell's website on cinema (blog)*, October 2. Accessed January 5, 2015. http://www.davidbordwell.net/blog/2007/10/02/vancouver-visions/.

Borg, Kristian. 2012. "Granskar vitheten på film." *Fria Tidningen*, March 8. http://www.fria.nu/artikel/92301.

Brodén, Daniel. 2013. "Den komplexa reklambilden: Om Roy Anderssons nydanande (kamera)inställning." In *I gränslandet: Nya perspektiv på film och modernism,* edited by Daniel Brodén and Kristoffer Noheden. Möklinta, Sweden: Gidlunds Förlag.

———. 2014. "Something Happened, but What? On Roy Andersson's Cinematic Critique of the Development of the Welfare State." In *Culture, Health and Religion at the Millennium: Sweden Unparadised*, edited by Marie Demker, Yvonne Leffler, and Ola Sigurdson, 99–132. New York: Palgrave McMillan.

Brogan, Terry V. F. 1993. "Anaphora." In *The New Princeton Encyclopedia of Poetry and Poetics*, edited by Alex Preminger and Terry V. F. Brogan, 73. Princeton: Princeton University Press.

Buber, Martin. 1965. "Guilt and Guilt Feelings." In *The Knowledge of Man: Selected Essays*, translated by Maurice Friedman and Ronald Gregor Smith, 121–48. New York: Harper & Row.

Byrnes, Paul. 2015. "How Sweden Hit Its 50:50 Gender Target for Film Production in Record Time." *The Sydney Morning Herald*, May 24. http://www.smh.com.au/entertainment/movies/how-sweden-hit-its-5050-gender-target-for-film-production-in-record-time-20150519-gh489a.html.

Céline, Louis Ferdinand. 1952. *Voyage au bout de la nuit*. Paris: Gallimard.

———. (1983) 2006. *Journey to the End of the Night*, translated by Ralph Manheim. New York: New Directions.

Chapple, Freda, and Chiel Kattenbelt. 2006. *Intermediality in Theatre and Performance*. Vol. 2. Amsterdam: Rodopi.

Clarke, Roger. 2008. "Reasons to Be Cheerful." *Sight and Sound* 18 (4): 34–36.

Cloarec, Eva. 2008. "Pernilla Sandström producerade Roy Anderssons film '*Du levande*.'" *Mitt i Botkryka/Salem*, 29. March 18. http://arkiv.mitti.se:4711/2008/12/botkyrka_salem/MIBO29A20080318SOV1.pdf.

Czouztornare, Aj. 1992. "The Day the Swiss Guard Was Massacred: The 1792 Tuileries Battle during the French Revolution." *Histoire* 156:79–81.

Dahlberg, Anna Bell. 1976. "Det har inte blivit mycket tid över för familjen." *Svenska Damtidning* 36:23.

Dahlén, Peter, Michael Forsman, and Klas Viklund. 1990. "Folkhemsdrömmen som sprack: Om den ironiska odramatiken i Roy Anderssons filmer." *Filmhäftet: Tidskrift om Film och TV* 69/70:33–44.

de Luca, Tiago, and Nuno Barradas Jorge, eds. 2015. *Slow Cinema*. Edinburgh: Edinburgh University Press.

Dempsey, Amy. 2002. *Styles, Schools and Movements*. London: Thames and Hudson.

Duffey, John Patrick. 2003. "El arte humanizado y la crítica cinematográfica de Jaime Torres Bodet y César Vallejo." *Anales de Literatura Hispanoamericana* 32:37–52.

Eberle, Matthias. 1985. *World War I and the Weimar Artists: Dix, Grosz, Beckmann, Schlemmer.* New Haven, CT: Yale University Press.

Ebert, Roger. 2002. "Songs from the Second Floor." RogerEbert.com, November 1. Accessed January 5, 2015. http://www.rogerebert.com/reviews/songs-from-the-second-floor-2002.

Edgar, Johan. 2001. "Moodysoon: Jag blev provocerad." *Expressen*, November 25.

Eggehorn, Ylva. 2004. "Kärlekens tid." In *BAO! Benny Anderssons Orkester med Helen Sjöholm.* CD. Stockholm: Mono Music.

Ekman, Stig, Klas Åmark, and John Toler. 2003. *Sweden's Relations with Nazism, Nazi Germany and the Holocaust: A Survey of Research.* Stockholm: Swedish Research Council.

Eriksson, Håkan. 2014. "Beckomberga sjukhus." *Bevara Stockholm* blog, March 4. Accessed January 15, 2015. http://bevarastockholm.blogg.se/2014/march/beckomberga-sjukhus.html.

Evry, Max. 2015. "Roy Andersson Reflects on 'A Pigeon Sits on a Branch Reflecting on Existence.'" Comingsoon.net, June 6. http://www.comingsoon.net/movies/features/447679-roy-andersson-reflects-on-a-pigeon-sat-on-a-branch-reflecting-on-existence.

Faldalen, Jon Inge. 2008. "'Är det någon som vet hur man kan ta sig härifrån?' En filmteoretisk stilstudie av den statiske innestellningens betydning i Roy Anderssons Sanger fra andre etasje." Master's thesis, University of Oslo.

"Filmmakers Live: Roy Andersson im Gespräch mit Ruben Östlund." 2011. Filmfest München. Accessed January 9, 2015. https://www.youtube.com/watch?v=nsCUTII3aT4.

Fonsmark, Anne-Birgitte, Marina Palà, and Rosa Puig Torres, eds. 2007. *Hammershøi i Dreyer / Hammershøi and Dreyer.* Spanish and English edition. Barcelona: Centre de Cultura Contemporània de Barcelona.

Fors, Mats. 1996. "Roy sjunger film igen." *Filmjournalen* 3:12–13.

Franco, Jean. 1976. *César Vallejo: The Dialectics of Poetry and Silence.* Cambridge: Cambridge University Press.

Girola, Fiammette, and Bruno Fornara, eds. 2003. *Roy Andersson.* Torre Boldone: Bergamo Film Meeting.

Gómez, Edward M. 2010. "A Haunting Humanism." *Art & Antiques* 33 (6): 64–73.

Göransson, Mattias. 2000. "Återkomsten." *Filmkonst* 69. Gothenburg, Sweden: Göteborg Film Festival.

Granath, Gunilla. 2000. "Samhället är inget soppkök." *Zoom* 12 (4): 10–11.

Grönkvist, Johanna. 2000. "Ingen gör svart film som inte tror på framtiden." *Filmjournalen* 3:18–19.

Hall, Margareta. 1975. "—Vadå, min film dålig? Jag *älskar* den!" *Damernas Värld* 49.

"Han är filmvärldens Zlatan." 2014. *Kulturprogrammet Sverige,* Swedish Television, September 8.

Hanich, Julian. 2014. "Complex Staging: The Hidden Dimensions of Roy Andersson's Aesthetics." *Movie: A Journal of Film Criticism* 5:37–50.

Hayward, Susan. 2006. "Avant-Garde." In *Cinema Studies: The Key Concepts,* edited by Susan Hayward. 38–40. New York: Routledge.

Hjort, Mette, and McKenzie, Scott, eds. 2003. *Purity and Provocation: Dogma 95.* London: British Film Institute.

Hjort, Mette, and Ursula Lindqvist. 2016. "Editors' Preface." In *A Companion to Nordic Cinema,* 1–12. Oxford: Wiley-Blackwell.

Hyltén-Cavallius, Charlotte, Birgitta Larsson, and Anna Lihammer. 2013. "Ett Annat Stockholm." *Stiftelsen Kulturmiljövård Skrifter* 4. Västerås, Sweden. Accessed July 28, 2015. http://www.kmmd.se/PageFiles/493/KM%20Skrifter%204_bwebben.pdf.

Jaffe, Ira. 2014. *Slow Movies: Countering the Cinema of Action.* New York: Wallflower Press.

Kääpä, Pietari. 2014. *Ecology and Contemporary Nordic Cinemas: From Nation-building to Ecocosmopolitanism.* New York: Bloomsbury.

Karhio, Anne. 2012. "Seamus Heaney, Paul Durcan and Hugo Simberg's 'Wounded Angel.'" *Nordic Irish Studies* 11 (1): 27–38.

Karlsson, Elise. 2013. "Beckombergas port öppnar sig på nytt." *Svenska Dagbladet*, August 17. Accessed June 20, 2015. http://www.svd.se/beckombergas-port-oppnar-sig-pa-nytt.

Kattenbelt, Chiel. 2008. "Intermediality in Theatre and Performance: Definitions, Perceptions, and Medial Relationships." In *Culture, Language and Representation* 6:19–29.

Kehr, Dave. 2010. "Direct Route to Lisbon Bypasses the Art House." *New York Times*, March 28.

Kiang, Jessica. 2014. "Venice Review: Roy Andersson's *A Pigeon Sat on a Branch Reflecting on Existence*." *The Playlist* (blog), Indiewire.com, September 2. http://blogs.indiewire.com/theplaylist/venice-review-roy-anderssons-a-pigeon-sat-on-a-branch-reflecting-on-existence-20140902.

Klinthage, Jörgen. 1991. "Behöll sin frihet i reklamfilmen." *Arbetet*, January 6.

Koskinen, Maaret. 2010. *Ingmar Bergman's "The Silence": Pictures in the Typewriter, Writings on the Screen*. Seattle: University of Washington Press / Museum Tusculanum.

Kostelantz, Richard. 1982. *The Avant-Garde Tradition in Literature*. Buffalo, NY: Prometheus Books.

Krutmeijer, Malin. 2014. "Bara så banalt!" *Helsingborgs Dagblad*, November 16. http://www.hd.se/kultur/2014/11/16/bara-sa-banalt/.

Lahger, Håkan. 2000. "En svensk filmarbetare: Lars Nordh." *Film & TV* 4:23–27.

Letmark, Peter. 2004. "Psykisk störning inget hinder för fängelse." *Dagens Nyheter*, February 12.

Lindqvist, Ursula. 2010. "Roy Andersson's Cinematic Poetry and the Specter of César Vallejo." *Scandinavian-Canadian Studies* 19:200–229.

———. 2016. "The Art of Not Telling Stories." In *A Companion to Nordic Cinema*, edited by Mette Hjort and Ursula Lindqvist, 547–565. Oxford: Wiley-Blackwell.

Lundblad, Kristina. 2000. "Vi är itusågade av Roy Andersson." *Göteborgs-Posten*, October 12.

Majsa, Barbara. 2015. "A Unique Universe: An Interview with Roy Andersson, István Borbás, and Gergely Pálos." *Cinema Scandinavia* 8 (Spring): 14–17.

Malmberg, Carl-Johan. 2000. "Hoppfull svartsyn i unikt mästerverk." *Svenska Dagbladet*, October 6.

Mannberg, Gustaf-Adolf. 1985. "Tystnad—Tagning: En intervju med Roy Andersson." *Resumé* 4.

Marx, Karl, and Frederich Engels. (1867) 1967. *Capital: A Critique of Political Economy Vol. 1*. New York: International Publishers.

Michalski, Sergiusz. 1998. *Neue Sachlichkeit: Malerei, Graphik und Photographie in Deutschland, 1919–1933*. Cologne: Taschen Verlag.

Mildren, Christopher. 2013. "Spectator Strategies, Satire and European Identity in the Cinema of Roy Andersson via the Paintings of Pieter Bruegel the Elder." *Studies in European Cinema* 10 (2/3): 147–55.

"1937 Munich Exhibition of Degenerate Art." United States Holocaust Memorial Museum website. Accessed January 15, 2015. http://www.ushmm.org/information/exhibitions/online-features/collections-highlights/julien-bryan/nazi-germany-1937/1937-munich-exhibition-of-degenerate-art.

Norén, Kjerstin. 2001. "Från IKEA till Cannes—tankar efter Roy Anderssons film *Sånger från andra våningen*." *Horisont* 48 (4): 36–41.

Oscarsson, Mattias. 2013. "Roy och hans värld." *Sydsvenskan*, January 20. http://www.sydsvenskan.se/kultur--nojen/roy-och-hans-varld/.

Oviedo Pérez de Tudela, Rocío. 2003. "La imagen diagonal: De lo cinemático en César Vallejo." *Anales de Literatura Hispanoamericana* 32:53–70.

Pallas, Hynek. 2012. "Vithet i svensk spelfilm, 1989–2010." PhD diss., Stockholm University.

Pham, Annika. 2007. "The Dark Side of 'The IKEA Life.'" Cineropa Film Focus, March 14. Accessed June 15, 2015. http://cineuropa.org/it.aspx?t=interview&l=en&did=74956.

———. 2014. "Philippe Bober: 'I'm Interested in Art with Content.'" *Nordisk Film & TV Fond*, September 19. Accessed June 15, 2015. http://www.nordiskfilmogtvfond.com/index.php/news/stories/philippe-bober-im-interested-art-content/.

Ratner, Megan. 2015. "The 'Trivialist' Cinema of Roy Andersson: An Interview." *Film Quarterly* 69 (1): 36-44.

Robinson, Tasha. 2012. "The Wachowskis Explain How *Cloud Atlas* Helps Unplug People from *the Matrix*." *A.V. Club*, October 25. Accessed January 6, 2015. http://www.avclub.com/article/the-wachowskis-explain-how-icloud-atlasi-unplugs-p-87900.

Romney, Jonathan. 2001. "Funny Peculiar." *Guardian*, February 8. http://www.theguardian.com/film/2001/feb/09/culture.features3.

Roos, Camilla. 2000. "Roy Andersson och blicken." *Filmjournalen* 2:11.

Runge, Björn, and Ulf Brantås. 1997. "Dokument rörande filmregissören Roy Andersson." *Eldsjälar: En dokumentärserie i fem delar*. Segment 3.

Russell, Dominique. 2008. "The Ghost of the Second Floor: Roy Andersson and César Vallejo." *Literature/Film Quarterly* 36 (4): 315-27.

Sanandaji, Nima. 2014. "Kvinnor i Sverige jobbar för få timmar." *Svenska Dagbladet*, November 11. http://www.svd.se/kvinnor-i-sverige-jobbar-for-fa-timmar.

Sandberg, Mark B. 2006. "John Gabriel Borkman's Avant-Garde Continuity." In *Modern Drama* 49 (3): 327–47.

Schmalenbach, Fritz. 1940. "The Term *Neue Sachlichkeit*." In *Art Bulletin* 22 (3): 164.

Sjögren, Hans. 2008. *Creating Nordic Capitalism: The Business History of a Competitive Periphery*. New York: Palgrave MacMillan.

Smith, Dennis. 1987. "Knowing Your Place: Class, Politics, and Ethnicity in Chicago and Birmingham, 1890–1983." In *Class and Space: The Making of Urban Society*, edited by Nigel Thrift and Peter Williams, 227–305. London: Routledge and Kegan Paul.

Smith, Jeremy. 2012. "Mr. Beaks Talks CLOUD ATLAS with Andy Wachowski, Lana Wachowski, and Tom Tykwer!" *Ain't It Cool* blog, October 24. http://www.aintitcool.com/node/59262.

Söderbergh Widding, Astrid. 2016. "How to Train a Director—Film Schools in the Nordic Countries." In *A Companion to Nordic Cinema*, edited by Mette Hjort and Ursula Lindqvist, 105–124. Oxford: Wiley-Blackwell.

Spigland, Ethan. 2010. "No Shadows to Hide In: A Conversation with Roy Andersson." *Orbis Mediologicus: The Project for Mediology at Pratt Institute*, September 12. https://orbismediologicus.wordpress.com/2010/09/12/no-shadows-to-hide-in-a-conversation-with-roy-andersson/.

Swedish Film Institute (SFI). 2013. "Riktlinjer filmkonsulenter." Accessed July 28, 2015. http://www.sfi.se/PageFiles/8465/Riktlinjer%20konsulenter_nya2013.pdf.

Tapper, Michael. 2002. "Folkhemmets svanesang." *Filmhäftet* 28 (3): 70–73.

Tatar, Maria. 1995. *Lustmord: Sexual Murder in Weimar Germany*. Princeton University Press.

Tec, Nechama, and Daniel Weiss. 1997. "A Historical Injustice: The Case of Masha Bruskina." *Holocaust and Genocide Studies* 11 (3): 366–77.

Tidningarnas Telegrambyrå (TT; Newspapers Telegram Bureau). 2000. "Roy Anderssons sågar s." *Göteborgs-posten*, November 23.

———. 2014. "Roy Andersson skissar på nästa film." *Svenska Dagbladet*, September 2. http://www.svd.se/roy-andersson-skissar-pa-nasta-film.

Timm, Mikael. 2003. *Dröm och förbannad verklighet: Spelet om svensk filim under 40 år*. Stockholm: Brombergs Förlag.

Triangelfilm. 2000. "Triangelfilm presenterar Roy Anderssons *Sånger från andra våningen*." Malmö, Sweden: Press Kit.

Ulaby, Neda. 2015. "Roy Andersson: From Mordant Ad Director to Philosophical Filmmaker." National Public Radio Weekend Edition, June 6. http://www.npr.org/2015/06/06/411989169/roy-andersson-from-mordant-ad-director-to-philosophical-filmmaker.

"Un Certain Regard Rendez-vous—Turist by Ruben Östlund." 2014. Cannes International Film Festival website, May 18. Accessed January 5, 2015. http://www.festival-cannes.fr/en/article/60953.html.

Utterström, Margareta. 1989. "Dags för långfilm av Roy Andersson." *Göteborgs-posten*, December 19.

Vallejo, César. 1974. *Mänskliga dikter [Human Poems]*. Translated by Marianne Sandels and Pierre Zekeli. Stockholm: FiB:s Lyrikklubb.

———. (1978) 1980. *César Vallejo: The Complete Posthumous Poetry*. Translated by Clayton Eshleman and José Rubia Barcia. Berkeley: University of California Press.

———. 1981. *César Vallejo: Uppfylld av världen* [Filled with the world]. Foreword by Artur Lundkvist. Translated by Peter Landelius, Francisco J. Uriz, Pierre Zekeli, and Marianne Sandels. Stockholm: Förlaget Nordan.

"Veckans gäst—Roy Andersson." 2014. *Kulturprogrammet Sverige*, Swedish Television, November 22.

Viklund, Klas. 2000. "En av de ljusaste filmerna på länge." *Zoom* 12 (4): 12.

Vishnevetsky, Ignatiy. 2009. "Figurative and Abstract: An Interview with Roy Andersson." *Notebook*. Accessed January 6, 2015. https://mubi.com/notebook/posts/figurative-and-abstract-an-interview-with-roy-andersson.

Wacquant, Loïc. 1996. "The Rise of Advanced Marginality: Notes on Its Nature and Implications." *Acta Sociologica* 39 (2): 121–39.

Weintraub, Steve. 2012. "Andy & Lana Wachowski & Tom Tykwer Talk CLOUD ATLAS, SPEED RACER, Test Screenings, Deleted Scenes, Favorite Movies & More." Collider blog, October 27. Accessed January 9, 2015. http://collider.com/andy-wachowski-lana-wachowski-cloud-atlas-speed-racer-interview/.

Weman, Mats. 1998. "Vem i helvete tror Roy Andersson att han är?!" *Film & TV* 4:20–30.

———. 2000a. "Sånger från andra våningen: Filmhandledning." *Zoom* 12 (4): 51–56.

———. 2000b. "Sånger från andra våningen." *Nöjesguiden*, October.

Wiberg, Charlotte. 2006. "Filmkritik i svensk dagspress—en ögonblickbild." *Solskenslandet: Svensk film på 2000-talet*, edited by Erik Hedling and Ann-Kristin Wallengren, 267–302. Stockholm: Atlantis.

Widerberg, Bo. 1962. *Visionen i svensk film*. Stockholm: Bonnier.

Wij, Tomas. 2001. "Lukasevangeliet." *Trots allt* 7/8:34–39.

Witoszek, Nina, and Lars Trägårdh, eds. 2002. *Culture and Crisis: The Case of Germany and Sweden*. New York: Berghahn Books.

World Economic Forum. 2014. *Global Gender Gap Report*. Accessed June 20, 2015. http://reports.weforum.org/global-gender-gap-report-2014/economies/#economy=SWE.

Yang, Julianne Qiuling Ma. 2012. "Towards a Cinema of Contemplation: Roy Andersson's Aesthetics and Ethnics." M.Phil. thesis, University of Hong Kong.

Zander, Ulf. 2003. "Holocaust at the Limits. Historical Culture and the Nazi Genocide in the Television Era." In *Echoes of the Holocaust: Historical Cultures in Contemporary Europe*, edited by Klas-Göran Karlsson and Ulf Zander, 255–92. Lund: Nordic Academic Press.

Zwick, Reinhold. 2008. "The Apocalypse of Andersson: Biblical Echoes in *Songs from the Second Floor*." In *Images of the Word: Hollywood's Bible and Beyond*, edited by David Shepherd. Atlanta: Society of Biblical Literature.

Unpublished Research Materials

"Faktisk Finansiering." Undated. Printed document listing the breakdown of funding sources for *Songs from the Second Floor*, provided to the author by Studio 24 producer Pernilla Sandström.

"Manuskript till filmprojektet 'Sånger från andra våningen' är under utarbetande och beräknas vara klart i mitten av december 1993." Undated. Draft of a funding proposal to the Swedish Film Institute, provided to the author by Roy Andersson.

"Sånger från andra våningen." 1993. Funding proposal on file in the Swedish Film Institute Library, Stockholm.

"Sånger från andra våningen (en existentiell komedi). Idébeskrivning och snopsis." Hand-dated November 1994. Draft of a funding proposal, provided to the author by Lisa Alwert.

"Scener i långfilmen 'Sånger från andra våningen' (preliminär ordningsföljd)." Undated. Document listing a preliminary order of scenes and scene descriptions, provided to the author by Roy Andersson.

Index

Ådalen 31 (Widerberg film), 17, 122
Adventurer, The (Chaplin film), 90
advertising films by Andersson, 8, 13, 14, 47, 64, 69, 122; awards for, 48; dramatic irony in, 145–46; LO—Arbete för alla, 169n19; for Lotto, 145; Why Should We Care About Each Other?, 144
All Things Fair (Lust och fägring stor) (Widerberg film), 165n17
Alonso, Lisandro: Los Muertos, 12
Alwert, Lisa, 27, 32, 51, 57, 58–59, 63, 65, 68–69, 151, 165n12
amateur actors, 10, 22, 51–52, 68–75
anaphora poetic device, 82
Andersson, Benny, 74, 83, 114–18, 136; "The Time of Love," 115–16
Andersson, Holger, 153
Andersson, Jan-Olov, 49, 145
Andersson, Jenny, 127
Andersson, Roy, 56; advertising films, 8, 13, 14, 47, 48, 64, 69, 122, 144, 145–46, 169n19; ambivalent relationship with Swedish film establishment, 15–17; anti-war stance, 7, 15, 105–6; artistic influences, 7, 36–37, 40, 68, 76–118; bankruptcy, 13; Bergman criticized by, 16–17; budget and schedule control, 46–47; building bought by, 13–14, 47; childhood dreams of becoming a painter, 51, 76, 96; childhood in Gothenburg, 14–15; close-ups rejected by, 20, 34; criticism, 10–11; dialogue modifications, 74; filmmakers influenced by, 11–12, 47–48, 52–53; filmmaking style traits, 10, 11–12, 33–44, 60–62, 121; films as three-dimensional paintings, 77–78; films previous to Songs, 12–13; gaps between films, 3, 151, 154; grant proposal rejections, 56–57, 63–64;

Andersson, Roy (*continued*)
"hidden dimensions" in works, 39, 102, 171n34; HIV virus origin viewed by, 172–73n8; honorary doctorate from the University of Gothenburg, 8; interest in Swedish folk music, 113–14; interviews, 23, 44, 97, 153; MoMA retrospective, 2009, 79, 169n8; musicality, 79, 114–15; *Our Time's Fear of Seriousness*, 5–6, 16, 17, 34, 114, 124, 126, 133, 147–48, 163n1; outdoor location shoots disliked by, 62; paradoxes of films, 5, 14, 17; political and class sympathies, 14–16, 24–25, 28–32, 41–42, 84–85, 92, 103, 105, 109–12, 119–23, 143–49; prizes awarded to, 164n13; as public intellectual, 119–20; set-building and -painting involvement, 52–55, 80, 96–97; set design, 7, 10, 42, 49–52, 96; short films, 48–49; societal critiques, 5–6, 121–32, 142–49; trivialist aesthetic, 23–24, 28, 32, 70–71, 78, 82, 85, 92, 94–95, 119; unconventional filmmaking methods, 46, 63–64, 72–74; unique vision of, 4–5, 9; use of whiteface, 26, 71; viewer activation by, 29–31, 39–40, 132–33. *See also specific films*
Andersson, Sten, 29
Antonioni, Michelangelo, 38
"aperture framing" technique, 40–41

Aréhn, Mats, 64
Arn: The Kingdom at the End of the Road (Flinth film), 164n11
Arn: The Knight Templar (Flinth film), 164n11
Aronofsky, Darren, 11, 153
ARTE, 65–66, 67
Aspelin, Tobias, 68
Auden, W. H.: "Musée des Beaux Arts," 95
avant-garde art, 7–8, 24

Balázcs, Béla: *The Theory of Film*, 33
Barcia, José Rubia, 170n22
Baum, L. Frank: *The Wizard of Oz*, 126
Bazin, André: "Charlie Chaplin," 90; "De Sica," 30; "The Evolution of the Language of Cinema," 36, 39; "Painting and Cinema," 80
Beatitudes, 88, 95
Beckett, Samuel: *Waiting for Godot*, 21–22, 44, 77, 81, 169n7
Beckomberga Hospital (Stockholm), 148–49, 174nn19–20
Beloved Are They Who Sit Down (Älskade vare de som sätter sig) (Andersson documentary project), 86
Benny Anderssons Orkester, 114, 116
Bergdahl, Gunnar, 47, 163n1
Bergman, Daniel: *Expectations*, 68
Bergman, Ingmar, 14; Andersson advertising films praised by, 48; Andersson's disagreements with, 15–17, 28; close-ups, 33; commercials

made by, 173n15; magician references in films, 42; *Persona*, 17; screenplay for *Faithless*, 4; *The Seventh Seal*, 17; *The Silence*, 17, 164n11; *Smiles of a Summer Night*, 164n15; *Winter Light*, 17

Bergman's Twentieth Century (documentary series), 16

Bicycle Thieves (Ladri di biciclette) (De Sica film), 14–15, 30

Bier, Susanne: *In a Better World*, 68

Bober, Philippe, 65–66, 67, 151

Bohlin, Britt, 121–22

Boman, Kalle, 8, 15, 56, 58, 79, 114, 147, 165n12

Borbás, István, 20, 39, 51–52, 53, 60, 61–62, 79, 87, 147, 153, 173n10

Bordwell, David: *Figures Traced in Light*, 6, 28, 39

Bothersome Man, The (Lien film), 8

Bourdieu, Pierre, 172n5

Brodén, Daniel, 119, 142–43, 145

Bruegel, Pieter, the Elder, 34, 78; *Hunters in the Snow*, 166n17; *Landscape with the Fall of Icarus*, 95–96

Bruskina, Masha, 137, *138*

Buber, Martin: "Guilt and Guilt Feelings," 18, 123, 133–34, 139

Buñuel, Luis, 33

Burrowing (Hellström/Wenzel film), 8

Cahiers du cinéma (journal), 33

Callot, Jacques: *The Hanging*, 36–37, *37*, 78, 95

Canal+, 66

Cannes International Film Festival (2000), 3–4, 66, 121, 150–51

Cannes International Film Festival (2014), 47–48

capitalism and neoliberalism critiqued by Andersson, 24–25, 30–31, 41–42, 45, 92, 123–32, 144, 147–49

Carlsson, Bengt C. W., 69, 168n33

Carlsson, Johan, 50–51, 53–54, 55, 58–59, 65, 122–23

Céline, Louis-Ferdinand, 18, 169n7; *Journey to the End of the Night*, 77, 81, 141–42

Chaplin, Charlie, 6–7, 88–90

Chaplin (journal), 16

Chekov, Anton, 24

Christell-Malmberg, Inger, 57

Church of Sweden, 146–47

cinematic mise-en-scène, 33–34

close-ups, 33–34

Colossal Youth (Costa film), 12

commodity fetishism, 85

"complex image" composition, 3, 6, 17, 34–39, 96–97, 102, 103

Computer Generated Images (CGI), 6

Co-Production Office (Copenhagen), 65–66

Costa, Pedro: *Colossal Youth*, 12

dadaists, 7

Dahl, Arne, 68

Dahlberg, Anna Bell, 12

Dahlén, Peter, 144

Dancer in the Dark (von Trier film), 151

Dardel, Nils, 79; *Execution*, 102–3, 104–5
Darling (Kling film), 26
Daumier, Honoré, 79
Decalogue (Kieślowski series), 24
deep-focus and wide-angle shots, 10, 34, 36, 38–40, 42, 57, 60, 72–73, 100, 102, 128–29
"Degenerate Art" exhibit (Munich, 1937), 171n39
De Sica, Vittorio: *Bicycle Thieves*, 14–15, 30
Dix, Otto, 78, 105–8; *To Beauty*, 106–7, 108–9; *Three Nudes on the Beach*, 106–7
"docufictional" filmmaking style, 11
Dogma 95, 8
dramatic irony, 6–7, 10, 145
Dreyer, Carl Th., 33, 40

Ebert, Roger, 5
Ecclesiastes, 77, 83, 126
Eggehorn, Ylva, 115
Eisenstein, Sergei, 35–36
Elvira Madigan (Widerberg film), 122, 165n17
Eshleman, Clayton, 170n22
Europa Films, 12–13
Eva & Adam (Swedish TV series), 68
Expectations (Svenska hjältar) (Bergman film), 68

Faithless (Trolösa) (Ullmann film), 4, 67
Fallström, Torbjörn, 29
Fellini, Federico, 24, 33
Ferrari, Américo, 82
film auteurs, 33
Film . . . (Surányi film), 167n10
Fincher, David: *The Girl with the Dragon Tattoo*, 168n33
fixed camera long takes, 9, 10, 11–12, 36, 38–40
Folkhemmet, 142–43, 173n14
Force Majeure (Turist) (Östlund film), 9, 47–48, 151
Förlaget Nordan, 81
Forman, Miloš, 24
Forsman, Michael, 144
Forum for Living History (Stockholm), 80, 120
Franco, Jean, 88–89, 170n25
Frankfurt School, 81

Gallen-Kallela, Akseli, 171n33
Giliap (Andersson film), 13, 46–47, 48, 50
Girl with the Dragon Tattoo, The (Fincher film), 168n33
Goering, Hermann, 38, 142
Gómez, Edward M., 106
Göransson, Bengt, 122
Göransson, Mattias, 3–4, 16, 145
Gothenburg Film Festival, 32, 65, 163n1
Goya, Francisco, 78
Grand Hôtel, Stockholm, 106, 112
Grönkvist, Johanna, 86
Grosz, George, 105–6
Grupp 13, 15
Guillou, Jan, 164n11
"guilt toward existence," 31, 95, 132–42

Guitar Mongoloid (Gitarrmongot) (Östlund film), 9
Guldbagge ("Golden Bug") Awards, 4
Gullberg, Hjalmar: "Scanian Castles and Manors," 113–14

Hamilton, G. H., 105–6
Hammershøi, Vilhelm, 40, 79
Hammershøi i Dreyer exhibition (Barcelona, Spain), 40
Hanich, Julian, 39, 102, 171n34
Hansson, Per Albin, 143
Härö, Klaus: *The New Man*, 68
Haydn, Joseph, 173n10
Hayward, Susan, 24
Hellström, Henrik: *Burrowing*, 8
Hitchcock, Alfred, 33
Hobbit trilogy (Jackson films), 68
Holocaust, 113–14, 120, 123, 126, 132–42
Hopper, Edward: *Automat*, 54, 57, 78
Humle, Kristina: *Love and Happiness*, 68

I Am Curious Blue (Jag är nyfiken bla) (Sjöman film), 122
I Am Curious Yellow (Jag är nyfiken gul) (Sjöman film), 122
In a Better World (Hævnen) (Bier film), 68
Iñárritu, Alejandro González, 11, 153
intermediality concept, 76–80
The Involuntary (De ofrivilliga) (Östlund film), 9

Jackson, Peter: *Hobbit* films, 68
Järegård, Ernst-Hugo, 70
Jarl, Stefan, 16; *They Call Us Hooligans*, 122
Jia Zhang-ke: *Still Life*, 11–12
Joe Hill (Widerberg film), 17, 122
Jonsson, Jens: *The King of Ping Pong*, 8

Kääpä, Pietari, 143–44
Kamprad, Ingvar, 70
Karhio, Anne, 97–98, 170n30, 170–71n33
Kattenbelt, Chiel, 77
Keaton, Buster, 6–7
Kehr, Dave, 11–12
Kiang, Jessica, 154
Kieślowski, Krzysztof: *Decalogue* series, 24
King, Martin Luther, Jr., 128
King of Ping Pong, The (Jonsson film), 8
Klevenås, Jesper, 51–52, 55, 60, 61–62, 77
Kling, Johan: *Darling*, 26
Kostelantz, Richard: "What Is Avant-Garde?", 7

Lahger, Håkan, 5, 12, 130
Landelius, Peter, 82
LännaAteljéerna Studio, 56–57
Larsson, Stefan, 57, 68–69, 70, 72–73, 74, 89, 149, 150
Lassgård, Rolf, 73
Last Sentence, The (Dom över död man) (Troell film), 168n33

Leigh, Mike, 11
lethargic pace, 6, 10
Lien, Jens: *The Bothersome Man*, 8
Lindgren, Astrid, 124; *Mio My Son*, 115
Lindh, Anna, 174n21
Love and Happiness (Krama mig) (Humle film), 68
Lundberg, Pia, 47, 148
Lundblad, Kristina, 26–27
Lundkvist, Artur, 82, 169n14
Lycka till och ta hand om varandra (Sjögren film), 168n33

Magnolia Pictures, 153–54
Magnusson, Leif: *Sidetracked*, 73
Malmberg, Carl-Johan, 130
Marx, Karl: *Capital*, 85
Mathiasson, Helene, 59, 109, 111, 140
Mayakovsky, Vladimir: "A Cloud in Trousers," 168n31
Méliès, Georges, 6, 42
Mészöly, Miklós, 167n10
Michalski, Sergiusz, 107
Mildren, Christopher, 35, 38, 39–40, 41, 106
Minsk public execution, 1941, 136–37, *138*
montage technique, 35–36
Moodysson, Lukas, 7–8; *Songs from the Second Floor* criticized by, 146; *Together*, 4, 67, 68
Mr. Moro Successfully Being Frozen in Cake of Ice (photograph), 173n16
Muertos, Los (Alonso film), 12

Munich Film Festival (2011), 34
Munter, Jens, 70
Museum of Modern Art (New York), 79, 169n8

National Public Radio (U.S.), 153
Nazis, 38, 113–14, 120, 126, 132–42, 171n39
neoliberalism. *See* capitalism and neoliberalism critiqued
Neue Sachlichkeit (New Objectivity), 7, 105–6, 108–9, 171n39
New Man, The (Den nya människan) (Härö film), 68
Nordh, Lars, 31–32, 57, 70, 71, 72, 73, 89, 122, 130, 146, 150

Of the Infinite (Om det oändliga) (Andersson film project), 154
Olsson, Klas-Gösta, 132–33, 141–42
Olsson, Sture, *140*
omkväde lyrical device, 82–83
Östlund, Ruben, 8–9, 12, 34; *Force Majeure*, 9, 47–48, 151; *Guitar Mongoloid*, 9; *The Involuntary*, 9; *Play*, 9
Overlooked Film Festival (2002), 5

Pallas, Hynek: *Vithet i svensk spelfilm 1989–2010*, 26
Persbrandt, Mikael, 68
Persona (Bergman film), 17
Persson, Edvard, 113–14
Pigeon Sat on a Branch Reflecting on Existence, A (Andersson film), 11, 43–44, 51, 151–54, 166n17

Play (Östlund film), 9

Rauer, Ann-Marie, 11
Renoir, Jean, 33
repetition as device, 11, 82–86, 118
Repin, Ilya, 79
Romney, Jonathan, 3
Roney, Shanti, 68
Roth, Peter, 87, 89
Russell, Dominique, 82, 94

Sandels, Marianne, 81
Sandrew Film & Teater, 13
Sandström, Pernilla, 27, 49, 62–63, 66, 164n11
Schein, Harry, 15–16
Serner, Anna, 27
set design, 7, 10, 42, 49–52, 96
Seventh Seal, The (Den sjunde inseglet), 17
Shcherbatsevich, Volodia, 137, 138
Shoulder Arms (Chaplin film), 90
Sidetracked (Villospår) (Magnusson film), 73
sight gags, 6–7, 10, 39–40, 88–90
Silence, The (Tystnaden) (Bergman film), 17, 164n11
silent cinema techniques, 6–7, 88–90
Simberg, Hugo, 79; *Wounded Angel*, 97–98, 99, 100–102
Sjögren, Fredrik, 136, 140
Sjögren, Hans, 143
Sjögren, Jens: *Lycka till och ta hand om varandra*, 168n33
Sjöholm, Helen, 115

Sjöman, Vilgot: *I Am Curious Blue*, 122; *I Am Curious Yellow*, 122
"slow cinema" movement, 11–12
Smiles of a Summer Night (Sommarnattens leende) (Bergman film), 164n15
Smith, Dennis, 130
Something Has Happened (Någonting har hänt) (Andersson unfinished short film), 113, 132, 172–73n8
Songs from the Second Floor (Andersson film): absence of editing within scenes, 6, 20; actors auditioned, 68–69; aesthetics, 19–44; amateur actors in, 22, 51–52, 68–75; analogic repetition in, 82–86, 85–86, 118; anticipation over, 3–4; art-historical images in, 78–79, 95–112; artistic influences on, 21–22, 68; awards, 4, 67, 121, 151, 163n2; between-take levity and camaraderie, 73; box-office receipts, 67; Cannes premiere, 150–51; church critiqued in, 146–47; color scheme and geometric use, 22–23, 88, 96, 124; complex images in, 3, 6, 34–39, 97, 102; contextualization, 18; crucifixes as commodity in, 131–32, 139; dialogue, 21–22, 74, 78, 84, 93–95, 100–101, 111–12, 131–32; director's commentary, 23–24; documentary on making of, 19; domestic distributor, 9, 64;

Songs from the Second Floor (Andersson film) *(continued)* DVD release, 67; early project description, 76–77; English-language press materials for, 9–10; epigraph, 76; expense, 64–65; festival presentation, 5; filming time and costs, 12, 150; financing, 49, 62–67; as first of trilogy, 11; foreign distribution deals, 65–66, 151; grant proposals for, 63–64; guilt in, 31, 95, 132–42; health-care system critiqued in, 146, 147–49, 174nn19–21; humanist ethos, 18, 43–44, 79–80, 119–49; influence of, 8; intellectual engagement demanded for, 122; intermediality in, 18, 76–118; lack of meaningful female roles in, 26–28; lighting, 60–61; literary and poetic influences, 76–77; medievalism in, 41, 110; musical repetition, 83, 118; music in, 74, 113–18, 128–29, 135–36, 152; naked or half-naked bodies seen in, 106–7; new film language of, 4–5, 18; pacing, 6; plot summary, 9–10; poetic superstructure, 82; production problems, 58–62; reception, 4–5, 7–8, 16, 26–27, 46, 49, 66–67, 121–22, 146; rejected idea of wandering poet, 86–87; reshoots, 96; sets built for, 49–52, 74–75; as social critique, 120–21, 123–32; specter of World War II in, 18; subsequent films, 151–54; as Sweden's Oscar entry, 4; thematic repetition, 83; title's meaning, 76, 113, 123, 153; verbal repetition, 83; viewer activation, 29–31, 39–40, 133; vignette structure, 10, 25–26; visual repetition, 83. *See also subcategories below*

Songs from the Second Floor (Andersson film) characters, 68–75; Anna, 59–60, 100–103, *101*, 105, 109–11, 115–16, 139, *140;* extras, 19–20, 31, 58, 61–62, 71; fake doctor, 89, *91;* hapless magician, 53, 91, 96, 117, *118;* immigrant, 93–94, 125–26, 148; Kalle, 31, 40–41, *42,* 45, *57,* 87–92, *89,* 113, 117, 128–29, 130–32, 135–39, *140,* 146–47, 149; Lasse, 28–31, *29,* 83, 86; Lennart, 69, 125–28; military colonel, 72–73, 132, 141–42; Pelle, 28–31, *29,* 42, 83, 84–86, 117, 126–27; psychologist, 27, 31, 100, 109–11, *111;* Queen Silvia, 100, *101,* 105, 115–16; reappearance of, 84; Robert, 42, 84–85, 117; Russian teen, 135–39, *140;* silent witnesses, 102, 115–16; Stefan, 41, *57,* 73, 74, 87–95, *89,* 116, 117, 118, 128, 129, 141, 149; Sven, 135–39, *140;* Tomas, 45, 87–95, *89,* 113, 118, 128, 148–49; Uffe, 131–32; use of Swedish nicknames for, 124–25

Songs from the Second Floor (Andersson film) locations: airplane hangar for train scene, 19–23, 22, 60; Gotland, 59–60, 103; Länna Ateljéerna Studio, 55–57, 57–58; Öland, 42, 59, 60–62; Storängsbotten Studio, 58

Songs from the Second Floor (Andersson film) scenes: "At the Dump—The Thousand Dead" final scene, 31, 38, 42, 49, 60–62, 120, 132, 139, *140*; bar scene, 55–57, 57–58, 64, 129–30; "The Bar" screen test 1, *55*; "The Bar" screen test 2, *56*; "Caught a Finger" (train station scene), 19–23, 22, 38–39, 60, *135*; "The Dumb Brother—The Corridor" scene, 58, 87–92, *89*, 113; emergency ward scenes, 34–35, 148; "The Fire Site" scene, 40–41, 58, 72; general's one-hundredth birthday scene, 38, 86, 132, 141–42, 149; general's one-hundredth birthday, scene aftermath, 38; hapless magician scene, 53, 96, 118; hapless magician scene aftermath, 117; immigrant beating scene, 125–26; Kalle's confession scene, 130–31; kitchen scene with Lasse, 83; kitchen scene with Stefan, 74, 116; "A Man is Fired" scene, 28–31, *29*; mental asylum scenes, 17, 45, 58, 87–95, 118, 128, 146, 148–49; "Misgivings I, Grand Hotel" scene, 74, 106, 107, 109–12, *111*; "Misgivings II, the Departure Hall" scene, 42, *43*, 58, 107, 127–28, 145; "The Oracle in the Solarium" opening scene, 83, 120, 126; Pelle and Robert bedroom scene, 84, 117; restaurant scene, 84–86; "The Sacrifice" scene, 31, 49, 59–60, 74–75, 86, 97, 98, 100–103, *101*, 105, 115–16; "The Sacrifice," scenes preceding, 100–103, 109–11; "The Scaffold in Minsk" scene, 135–37, *136*; sitting-down scene sequence, 84–85; stockbroker self-flagellation scene, 17, 41–42, 72; subway scene, 64, 116–17, 128–29; taxi scene, 41, 72–73; trade fair scene, 131–32; train station café scene, 137–39

Stenfeldt, Eva, 48, 52, 70, 72, 74–75, 109–11, *111*

Still Life (Jia film), 11–12

Storängsbotten Studio, 58

Strindberg, August: *A Dream Play*, 77, 81, 169n7, 172n7

Studio 24: design for *Sweden and the Holocaust* living history exhibition, 80, 120; expansion of, 58; independence of, 13–14, 50–51; in-house production staff, 49; interns, 8, 51; location of, 13, 113; management and financing, 62–67; original sets built by, 49–62; payment of amateur actors, 71–72; production crew problems, 58–62

Successful Freezing of Mr. Moro (Lyckad nedfrysning av Herr Moro) (anthology), 60, 79, 120, 147, 173n16
Sundström, Stefan, 68
superstructure of Andersson's films, 9, 10, 25–26, 35, 82
Surányi, András: *Film . . .*, 167n10
surrealists, 7
Svensk Filmindustri, 47
Sweden: Church's role in, 146–47; economic crisis of 1990s, 103, 105, 126–27; film industry in, 13–14, 45–49, 63–67; gender equality policies, 27; health-care system critiqued by Andersson, 146, 147–49, 173n16, 174nn19–21; as purported collaborator with Nazis, 113–14, 120, 126, 139–41; welfare society in, 24–25, 26, 119, 121–22, 123, 127–28, 142–49
Swedish Film Institute (SFI), 4, 15, 27, 63–64, 65, 67
Swedish Love Story, A (Andersson film), 4, 12, 46, 48, 119

Tarkovsky, Andrei, 33, 38
Tatar, Maria, 106
Tec, Nechama, 137
They Call Us Hooligans (Dom kallar oss mods) (Jarl documentary), 122
Together (Tillsammans) (Moodysson film), 4, 67, 68
Triangelfilm, 9–10, 64

trivialist aesthetic: in Andersson's films, 23–24, 28, 32, 70–71, 78, 85, 119; in Vallejo's poetry, 82, 92, 94–95
Troell, Jan: *The Last Sentence*, 168n33
trompe l'oeil technique, 6, 10, 42–43, 60, 63
Two Brothers and a Sister (Två bröder och en syster) (Andersson film project), 13

Ullmann, Liv: *Faithless (Trolösa)*, 4, 67
University College of Film, Radio, Television and Theatre (Stockholm), 164–65nn15–16
University of the Arts (Stockholm), 164–65nn15–16
urban marginalization, 123–32

Vallejo, César, 18, 77, 78, 169n7, 170n22; *Human Poems (Poemas humanos)*, 82, 89–90; poetry translated into Swedish, 81–82; "Stumble between Two Stars," 68, 82, 86–95, 102, 115
Venice Film Festival (2014), 11, 15, 152, 154
Viklund, Klas, 144
von Trier, Lars: *Dancer in the Dark*, 151
Vucina, Lucio, 145

Wachowski, Lana, 11, 24, 52–53

Wacquant, Loïc, 123–25, 172n5; "The Rise of Advanced Marginality," 124, 130
Wallenberg, Gustaf Oscar, 103
Weimar Republic, 105–6
Weiss, Daniel, 137
Weman, Mats, 3, 46, 47
Wenzel, Fredrik: *Burrowing*, 8
Westblom, Nils, 153
White Sport, The (Den vita sporten) (Swedish documentary), 15
Wiberg, Charlotte, 121
wide-angle shots. *See* deep-focus and wide-angle shots
Widerberg, Bo, 15; *dalen 31*, 17, 122; *All Things Fair*, 165n17; *Elvira Madigan*, 122, 165n17; *Joe Hill*, 17, 122; *Vision in Swedish Film*, 17
Wilson, Roger, 11
Winter Light (Nattvärdsgästerna) (Bergman film), 17
World of Glory (Andersson short film), 65, 132–33, *134*, 141
Wright, Georg Henrik von: "Humanism as an Attitude to Life," 120

You, the Living (Du Levande) (Andersson film), 11, 63, 67, 151, 152–53

ZDF, 66
Zekeli, Pierre, 81
Zwick, Reinhold, 67, 117–18, 120–21, 124–25, 126, 127–28, 131, 147

www.ingramcontent.com/pod-product-compliance
Lightning Source LLC
Chambersburg PA
CBHW011954150426
43198CB00020B/2928